Evaluating

Concepts for all levels

the Impact

Evaluation methods and practices

# of Training

Gaining management support

A Collection of Tools and Techniques

FOREWORD BY

DONALD L. KIRKPATRICK

BY SCOTT B. PARRY

ASTD

TABLE OF CONTENTS

FOREWORD

Scott Parry's book can best be described as practical, challenging, and extensive. In addition to clarifying the Kirkpatrick Four-Level Model, he consistently goes far beyond that by providing tools and techniques for the evaluation of training.

I like the way the book is oriented to the learner. Each chapter begins with the challenge: "Upon completing this chapter, you should be able to . . ." This illustrates his concern for the learner and the assurance that the learner has read and understood the chapter.

He makes it clear in his introduction that it is not necessary to read all of the chapters. Each chapter is briefly described and learners can select those that would be of special interest and benefit.

The last part of the book will be of special interest to those who are familiar with the Kirkpatrick Model. As I did in Part II of my book, *Evaluating Training Programs: The Four Levels,* Parry has devoted the last chapters to case studies of application. These can be studied to borrow or adapt ideas for forms and procedures for doing your own evaluation.

One extra that Parry has included is how to communicate the results of evaluation to higher management in order to get support and, perhaps, save your job when and if reengineering or downsizing takes place.

I strongly recommend this book for anyone interested in evaluation.

Donald L. Kirkpatrick
Author: *Evaluating Training Programs: The Four Levels*

About the Author

Scott B. Parry is a psychologist, consultant, trainer, and chairman of Training House, Inc., creators of instructional programs and assessments. His Managerial Assessment of Proficiency (MAP) has been translated into five languages and is used throughout the world.

He has published numerous articles in the training and management journals, and is the author of four books and dozens of published training courses. To date, he has run more than 400 "Train the Trainer" workshops and has addressed HRD conferences in several dozen countries.

In private life, Scott Parry plays the organ and harpsichord, has published three collections of music, and has given a carillon concert tour in Europe. He and his wife live in Princeton, New Jersey.

HOW TO USE THIS BOOK

This book is a resource—a collection of tools and techniques for evaluating training programs. Its 26 lessons typically begin with instruction, followed by examples: assessments, case studies, checklists, worksheets, evaluation forms (rating sheets). These instruments illustrate how different methods of evaluation have been applied to a variety of organizations and areas of training.

While there is a logic and flow to this book, its main value to you does not depend on being read from cover to cover (unless you're an incurable insomniac looking for a palliative). A detailed table of contents should make it easy for you to find what you need and to read selectively.

Here's what we suggest. Read the first 10 chapters, since they deal with concepts that apply to all types and levels of evaluation: the Kirkpatrick model; feasibility analysis; learning objectives vs. workplace expectations; transfer of training; workplace reinforcers and constraints; reliability and validity.

Chapters 11 through 24 deal with evaluation methods that are appropriate to the different levels you select for evaluation. Specifically, they are as follows:

Chapters 11-12	Level 1: Reaction	Did trainees like it?
Chapters 13-16	Level 2: Learning	Did trainees learn it?
Chapters 17-19	Level 3: Behavior	Did trainees use it?
Chapters 20-22	Level 4: Results	Did training pay (ROI)?
Chapters 23-24	Evaluating the instructor and the course design	

Finally, chapter 25 contains guidelines for preparing reports and a "success story" that can be use to publicize the effectiveness of your training efforts and to win support from senior management. Chapter 26 contains a self-assessment for you to evaluate your own strength on six instructional competencies.

Evaluation should be done both before and after training, with a dual focus of improving individual performance and meeting organizational goals and standards. Fortunately, many of the tools and techniques illustrated in this book are appropriate to all four of the situations that are summarized in the table on the next page.

	PRETRAINING	**POSTTRAINING**
Individual Evaluations	◆ to make sure the right trainees enroll for the right courses ◆ to arouse interest by showing trainees their strengths and needs ◆ to determine performance levels so as to measure gain after training	◆ to certify, qualify, or license certain types of jobholders ◆ to identify needs for further training, coaching, development ◆ to measure improvement due to training and give feedback
Organizational Evaluations	◆ to offer courses that are relevant to major needs of the organization ◆ to serve as a blueprint for course design (training needs analysis) ◆ to provide a benchmark against which we measure improvement	◆ to revise or drop courses based on their organizational impact ◆ to justify or modify the budget for training and development ◆ to qualify for industrywide awards (for example, Baldridge, ISO 9000)

A word about the instruments used in these chapters. They are protected by copyright, having been developed for publication or for use within client organizations of Training House.

I've enjoyed assembling and describing the tools and techniques in this collection. If you find this resource book helpful, then we'll both have benefited from the experience.

Scott B. Parry
Princeton, NJ

CHAPTER 1

WHY WE EVALUATE

Upon completing this chapter you should be able to

- ◆ identify at least four factors affecting the success of a training program
- ◆ describe the gap between entering behavior (EB) and terminal behavior (TB)
- ◆ list at least five things to be evaluated before launching a training program
- ◆ state at least three factors to be evaluated during training
- ◆ identify at least four factors to be evaluated after training
- ◆ describe the four levels (Kirkpatrick) at which training can be evaluated
- ◆ give several examples of training you would not evaluate at Levels 3 or 4
- ◆ list at least six benefits of evaluating training.

A study released by the American Society for Training and Development (ASTD) in 1996 identified as a key issue for the new millennium the need to measure performance improvement related to training. This comes as no surprise. Top management wants to know what results the organization is getting from the hundreds of thousands of dollars spent annually in training. Instructors and course designers want to know what impact their programs are having on individuals and the organization. Trainees and their supervisors want to know what kind of payoff they can expect from taking time away from productive work to participate in a course. In short, the evaluation of training's impact is a hot topic.

A training program is most successful when the right participants (selection) receive the right knowledge, attitudes, and skills (KAS, or content) taught by means of the right methods, media, and instructor (process) at the right time (need to know) and place (location) so as to meet or exceed the organization's expectations (learning objectives and performance outcomes).

Evaluating Before You Train

Our job would be much easier if the evaluation of training's impact were a binary issue. But it's not. We're not concerned simply with whether or not we hit the target. Rather, our evaluation of impact should yield insights into such things as which course objectives need more work; where we have been successful; and where we can improve (on design, delivery, content, length of course, selection of participants). That's why we should evaluate each of the factors listed in the preceding paragraph before a training program is launched.

Putting it another way, the evaluation process should begin with the needs analysis that precedes training. Indeed, we might define training as the process of closing the KAS gap between what our trainees bring to the course (their entering behavior, or EB) and what they must leave with to perform effectively at work (their terminal behavior, or TB). Since the purpose of training is to close this EB-TB gap, we'd better know the nature and size of this gap and the factors that will help or hinder our efforts to close it. Here, then, are some of the things we might want to evaluate before we start to design, develop, or deliver a training program:

- ◆ What do our learners want to know and expect to get from the training?
- ◆ What do our learners need to know and must get from the training?
- ◆ What competencies are required of learners? What prerequisite EB?
- ◆ What workplace factors will help or hinder the desired performance?
- ◆ What outcomes (TB) are expected? Realistic? Desirable? Measurable?
- ◆ What is the nature and size of the gap between EB and TB?
- ◆ What resources exist (people, equipment, supplies) to facilitate learning?
- ◆ What are the costs of training relative to the estimated benefits?

The answers to these and other similar questions will lead to decisions on how to make or buy the training program that will be most successful in closing the EB-TB gap. We also may be able to take actions to improve the workplace and make it more supportive of the desired TB, since many kinds of performance problems cannot be corrected by training.

Evaluating During Your Training

We've just examined some of the factors to be evaluated before training. Now let's look at some of the things you might want to evaluate during training so that you can take appropriate action when necessary and not wait until the course is over and it's too late:

- Are your participants comfortable? Assess seating, lighting, temperature, ventilation, breaks, pacing, mixture of theory and practice (acquisition and application, or hands-on learning).

- Are your participants learning? Use criterion tests and short quizzes to evaluate their acquisition, and practice exercises to assess their soft skills (role play, simulation) and their technical skills (at a PC or on the equipment).

- Is your content relevant? Can your participants relate the new KAS to their own needs? Can they provide examples of its practical application in their jobs? Are they active or passive throughout the course?

- Is the training enjoyable? Learning is much more effective and transfer of training from workshop to workplace is more complete when your learners enjoy the experience and contribute to its success with good participation.

Evaluating After You Train

Most participants are familiar with the end-of-course "smile sheet" that evaluates their reaction to the course. Some training programs also have a mastery test to measure how well participants have learned the material. This type of assessment is required in courses that lead to certification or licensing as a prerequisite to holding a job or performing certain kinds of tasks. Such evaluations are usually done immediately after the training.

The increased emphasis on performance in the workplace and return-on-investment (ROI), however, has led trainers to evaluate their impact months after a course is over. Only then can we get true measures of how well our graduates are dealing with the reinforcers and constraints of the workplace—the factors that help or hinder employees as they attempt to apply what they learned. Only then can we evaluate transfer of training. Here are some of the questions we might want to answer as we collect data during our evaluation of performance of our graduates at work:

- To what degree are our graduates meeting the desired TB?
- What factors are helping or hindering their performance?
- What can be done to strengthen the reinforcers and reduce the constraints?
- What aspects of our training proved to be most and least relevant?
- What changes in performance can be seen from pretraining to posttraining?
- What is the dollar value of these changes?
- How does the value of the improvements compare with the cost of training?

This list of questions reminds us that there are many factors influencing the effectiveness of training that can best be measured after some time has elapsed following the training program. But how much time? Are we talking about weeks, months, or years? The answer is critical if we plan to do an accurate cost-benefit analysis to measure the ROI. And here we have both good news and bad.

The good news is that the more times a training program is run, the greater will be the number of graduates. The costs of running a course are usually known in advance, before the first cycle is launched: conducting the needs analysis, selecting or creating the course, running the field tests, making revisions, reproducing the materials. These are fixed, one-time costs. In contrast, the benefits are variable as a function of (a) how many people are trained over the life of the course, and (b) how long each graduate will be able to use the new learning on the job (the payback period). This usually means that by waiting until a course has been conducted many times and run through its life cycle, we will have trained the largest number of employees who can yield a return on the initial investment. We will have increased our chances of getting the best ROI possible.

The bad news is that the longer we wait to evaluate performance in the workplace attributable to training, the larger will be the influence of intervening variables—factors that have nothing to do with the quality of our training but that affect performance and make it impossible for us to tell what behavior is and isn't attributable to training. Some examples are changes in technology; management; systems and procedures; organizational priorities and objectives; and the composition of the workforce.

In courses where innovation and technology lie at the core of the training, the life expectancy and payback period of a course may be measured in months. But in courses dealing with skills and competencies that should last a lifetime, the payback period will cover years. Such courses include leadership, team building, project management, writing skills, interpersonal communications, problem solving, negotiation, and conflict management. Isn't it ironic that many of the so-called soft skills courses have a longer payback period than many of the high-tech courses that are very situational, specific, and often "here today, gone tomorrow."

Evaluating at Four Levels

We've just examined the things we might want to evaluate before, during, and after running a training program. We've looked at many questions to be answered at each of these three phases of human resources development (HRD). Now let's turn our attention to the four levels at which training can be evaluated. And here we are indebted to Donald Kirkpatrick of the University of Wisconsin for the model he developed almost 40 years ago. A complete explanation can be found in his book, *Evaluating Training Programs* (San Francisco: Berrett-Koehler, 1994). Here are the four levels of the Kirkpatrick model:

LEVEL	ISSUE	QUESTION ANSWERED	TOOL
1	Reaction	How well did they like the course?	Rating Sheets
2	Learning	How much did they learn?	Tests, Simulations
3	Behavior	How well did they apply it at work?	Performance Measures
4	Results	What return did the training investment yield?	Cost–Benefit Analysis

Here's another way of depicting the four-level model. As you study it, think about several of the training programs with which you are familiar. For each one, recall the levels at which the impact is and isn't being evaluated. Then return to the observations noted below.

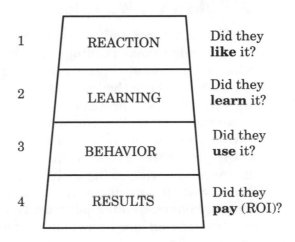

Data is easiest to generate at the top of the model and progressively harder to collect and to interpret (that is, attribute to training) as we go down the model. The effects being measured are short range at the top of the model and progressively longer range as we descend (that is, more permanent and more delayed before we can observe and measure them). Estimates indicate that over 85% of all training programs are evaluated at Level 1. This number drops progressively as we descend, with fewer than 10% being measured at Level 4.

These observations should not surprise us. Levels 1 and 2 are concerned with the learner's behavior in class or upon completion of the training. Thus, they can usually be measured by relatively simple paper-and-pencil exercises: end-of-course evaluation sheets for Level 1, and mastery tests for Level 2. Such instruments are relatively easy to create, to administer, and to interpret (tally, score, summarize).

In contrast, Levels 3 and 4 are concerned with the learner's behavior after the training is over—sometimes long after, as in courses on Selection Interviewing or Performance Appraisal or Selling to a Multinational Client, where it may be months or years before the trainee has a chance to apply what was learned in class. Although trainers attempt to apply the just-in-time concept and want to offer their programs at a time and place that enables learners to take courses just before they need them, this is virtually impossible to do in most organizations. Thus, any failure to get satisfactory results when we evaluate at Levels 3 and 4 may be attributable to the decay due to time lapse (a natural consequence of all training and education) and not to any inadequacy on the part of the learner, the instructor, or the course design.

Self-instructional courses via text or computer or interactive video (computer-based training, touch screen or "info-window") can help to overcome the delay factor by making training available when the learner needs it rather than when the instructor and organization offer it. But self-study has its limits with learners who need the personal touch and with courses that require hands-on learning or interaction with other learners (role plays, case method, games or simulation, PC operations, lab work).

Workshop vs. Workplace

The instructor and course designer have a pure environment in class or self-study to take readings at Levels 1 and 2. The learners are captive, relatively free of workplace distractions, and usually motivated to learn— or at least to keep the instructor happy enough to get through the training without hassle or incident.

In contrast, their performance back in the workplace (as measured by Levels 3 and 4) is influenced by many variables not addressed in class. They operate in a contaminated environment, and no one can control the intervening variables (or even hold them constant or equate for them) so that we might attribute the learner's performance to training alone. Rather, behavior on the job must be attributed to the whole array of factors influencing how people perform at work. Here are 10 of these factors, although the list is by no means exhaustive:

1. relevancy of what was taught to what is needed to perform
2. immediacy of opportunity to apply (discussed earlier)3. supportiveness of immediate supervisor of the learner
3. degree to which peers practice what the learner is trying to apply
4. time, money, and resources to support the new behavior
5. rewards and punishments that reinforce behavior
6. agreement of equipment and procedures between workshop and workplace
7. culture focused on long-range performance
8. workplace free of distractions, interruptions, and physical constraints
9. immediacy and specificity of feedback.

When To Measure at Levels 3 and 4

Although the list above might be enough to discourage the staunchest trainer from going beyond the use of smile sheets and end-of-course tests, there are a number of situations in which the behaviors elicited in class are virtually identical to the performance required on the job. In other words, environmental contamination is minimal. In such cases, Level 3 and 4 data may be relatively easy to obtain. Courses that deal with the following are examples:

- safety/drugs/alcohol (number of occurrences before and after training)
- data processing (order entry, inventory control)
- assembly line procedures (soldering, crimping, screwing, gluing)
- processing of paperwork (bank tellers, insurance claims processors)
- customer service (representatives behind desk in banks, airports, hotels)

These jobs are ones where "the rubber hits the road," where it is possible to measure the quantity and quality of output—number of transactions per hour, number of errors (rejects, overages or shortages, reworks) per 1,000 units or transactions, and so on.

Let's look at another type of job where Level 3 and 4 measurement might be feasible: persons who have a high degree of control over how their time is spent, and whose work is relatively independent of direct supervision or the intervention of other employees. Again, here are some examples:

- salespersons on commission (real estate, insurance, manufacturer's representatives)
- trades and crafts (electrician, plumber, carpenter)
- creative work (computer programmers, designers, writers, consultants)
- truck delivery (route drivers, postal service, messengers or couriers)

As we look over the types of jobs in which the 10 factors listed earlier are present or absent, we come to several conclusions. The following serve as general guidelines in deciding whether or not to measure at Levels 3 and 4:

1. The farther down the organization chart you are training, the easier it is to collect data on performance at work and its impact on the organization's mission and bottom line. Conversely, the farther up you go (supervisory, managerial, executive), the harder it is to quantify and to observe output.

2. The more directly responsible employees are for their own output and the more influence they have over the variables affecting output (line jobs vs. staff jobs, producing goods vs. services), the easier it is to go to Levels 3 and 4.

3. The more control employees have over how they spend their time (service repair, taxi driver, consultant), the more accountability they have for demonstrating results and ROI at Level 4.

4. The more direct influence an employee's performance has on earnings (commissions, bonus, incentives), the greater the likelihood that the employee will work extremely hard at overcoming workplace factors—our list of 10—that get in the way of outstanding performance (sales commissions, stock options, profit sharing).

When To Skip Levels 3 and 4

To the results-oriented manager or owner who is attracted to Adam Smith's economics, there's a certain appeal to the argument that Levels 1 and 2 don't count: "We're not paying employees to like the course or, for that matter, to learn. We're paying them to perform, and training has added no value to the organization until it can demonstrate that it produced improved performance in the workplace and contributed to the attainment of our mission and objective—a return on the investment."

There are several fallacies to this argument. They are identified by the four "facts" that follow. When these facts are present in your training programs, it may mean that you should either skip data collection in the workplace or settle for opinions of impact (subjective and soft data) rather than measures of performance (objective and hard data).

Fact A: Some workplace behaviors cannot be measured objectively. We teach supervisors how to do performance appraisals that are constructive, interactive, supportive, focused on performance rather than personality, and legal. But how can the course's impact be measured? We cannot observe our graduates as they conduct appraisals; it's a rather private affair. Even if both parties agreed willingly to be observed, the presence of an observer would contaminate the appraisal, and we would not get a reliable reading. True, we might examine the comments entered on the appraisal form after the review, assuming we get permission. This might show us whether our supervisors have focused on performance rather than on personality. But we are still left without any objective measure of the review itself. So we can try for subjective, soft data (by surveying supervisors and their employees, getting their opinions on pretraining and posttraining behavior during reviews). Or we can abandon attempts to measure at Levels 3 and 4.

Fact B: Some workplace behaviors may never occur. Examples include how to give artificial respiration; how to operate a fire extinguisher; how to use karate or jujitsu on an assailant; how to handle a bank holdup; how to terminate an employee; how to evacuate a 727 airplane in a water landing; how to tow a drowning person to shore; how to manage a nuclear power plant reactor in a crisis. The ultimate example, of course, is military training. Governments spend billions of dollars annually training the armed services to perform complex operations under combat conditions that, God willing, they will never have to do. In all of these situations, the usual way to assess at Level 3 is to create simulations—a sort of fail-safe approximation of the real thing. But the trainees know it isn't real, and the emotional response is very different.

Fact C: Some workplace behaviors cost too much to measure. We teach supervisors how to do selection interviews. We could follow up by sending a professional evaluator (consultant or psychologist) as a job applicant to each trained supervisor who had a job opening during the three months following training (along with actual applicants, of course, that the personnel department would screen and provide). But this would be expensive, time consuming, and lead to questions of ethics and appropriateness. What if supervisors find out that they are being "shopped," for example? What effect will this have on their level of trust in training and HRD? Another example is the use of assessment labs before and six months after supervisory training. While this might be an excellent way to measure impact, the cost would be prohibitive.

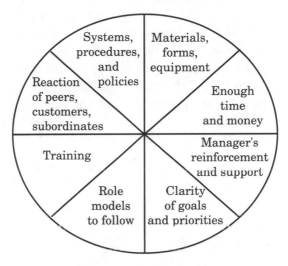

Factors Affecting Performance

Fact D: Most workplace behaviors cannot be attributed to training alone. In our earlier list of factors influencing performance, we made this point. When behavior is significantly better following a course, trainers are quick to take credit. When it isn't, we cite all the workplace factors that intervened (much like the advertising agency that claims credit for an ad campaign when sales go up, but cites recessionary trends and a flat economy when sales fail to result). The pie diagram above reminds us that the training employees receive is but one factor affecting their performance. The size of each wedge differs with each course and each job. The larger the influence of other wedges relative to the size of the training wedge, the harder (and more dangerous) it is for trainers to attribute workplace performance to workshop efforts.

Value-Added Assessment

We have now come to the realization that often the results of training can't be measured (facts A and B), cost too much to measure (fact C), or can't be attributed to training (fact D). This should not lead us to abandon training anymore than the absence of a viable means of measuring the impact of religion on the quality of life (personal and societal) should lead us to close churches. Although we cannot document the impact of its presence, evaluating the impact of its absence is a far less desirable option. As the saying goes, "If you think education is expensive, try ignorance!" But, this approach avoids evaluation altogether. So let's examine another approach—one that borrows the value-added concept from the field of economics and looks at the stages a learner goes through during the course of a training program.

First we need a definition of value-added assessment. In economics, value is added to a final product or service each time an operation is performed. Consider a loaf of bread on your table. The first value was added when the farmer grew wheat. The miller ground the wheat into flour. The baker converted flour and other ingredients into bread. And the truck delivered the loaf to your home or a store. Value was added at each stage. In many societies, each contributor pays a value-added tax proportional to the contribution and its impact on final value. The ultimate consumer pays a price for bread that is the sum of all these individual contributions of value. In the chart that follows, we've described the value that is added to a training program at each of the four levels of evaluation, along with suggestions as to how this value can be assessed.

FOUR LEVELS OF EVALUATION

Let's apply this rationale to the evaluation of training each time an operation is performed. In the chart below, four operations are listed in the sequence in which they occur throughout the life of a course. We've identified the value-adding components of each, along with a description of how the value added might be assessed.

	OPERATION	VALUE-ADDING COMPONENTS	HOW ASSESSED
LEVEL 1: REACTION	A course is researched, designed or selected, and presented.	◆ needs analysis conducted ◆ instructional design and development ◆ course materials ◆ instructor's delivery skills ◆ learning facilities ◆ program time and timing ◆ selection of participants	Evaluation sheets measure learners' reactions to: content, relevancy, use format, methods, media readability, graphics, image pacing, clarity, fun comfort, location, meals when offered, length homogeneity, networking
LEVEL 2: TRAINING	Subject matter (course content, KAS) is delivered to learners.	◆ Knowledge is imparted (facts, rules, procedures, policies, concepts, theory) ◆ Attitudes are shaped (values, perceptions, beliefs, styles, feelings) ◆ Skills are practiced to develop competence and confidence (many types of skills: perceptual, verbal, cognitive, manual, psychomotor)	Learners are evaluated throughout training to see how well they are acquiring KAS; end-of-course mastery test is used if appropriate.
LEVEL 3: BEHAVIOR	Learners translate workshop behavior into workplace performance.	Improvement in individual data: ◆ quantity of work ◆ quality of work ◆ shorter time to reach competency	Learner's output is measured; evaluation by self or others; performance in simulations or activities done off line (in an assessment lab).
LEVEL 4: RESULTS	The organization reaps the harvest of improved workplace performance.	Improvement in organizational data: ◆ overall productivity of plant, department ◆ market share ◆ profitability ◆ work teams without supervision ◆ reduced cost of lawsuits, insurance claims, lost business, accidents, turnover	Cost-benefit analysis or pretraining and posttraining comparison of data already in the system (accident rate, new accounts, rejects, absenteeism, turnover within 90 days).

The Benefits of Evaluating

In this chapter we've examined the kinds of data to be collected and evaluated before, during, and after conducting a training program. We've also examined the four levels at which training can be evaluated (reaction, learning, behavior, results), along with guidelines for deciding which levels are and aren't appropriate for different kinds of courses. Now let's summarize with a list of benefits—reasons why you should evaluate the impact of your training programs more rigorously:

◆ To find out where the desired expectations (goals) are and aren't being met

◆ To make the training environment more supportive of learning

◆ To revise and refine the course to make it more effective

◆ To identify and reduce workplace constraints that inhibit transfer

◆ To prove that training doesn't cost; it pays (an investment vs. expense)

◆ To win commitment and support of training by management

◆ To give instructors and course developers feedback to help them improve

◆ To justify and perhaps enlarge the training budget

◆ To influence future decisions on what kinds of courses to run

◆ To manage the training function more professionally.

Chapter 2

Doing a Feasibility Analysis

Upon completing this chapter you should be able to

- give at least three benefits of doing a feasibility analysis
- list at least seven questions that a feasibility analysis should answer
- describe at least three reasons for not doing a feasibility analysis
- state at least four measurable benefits of using preworkshop questionnaires
- describe how a pretraining list of course objectives might be used.

Did you ever hear this expression: "It's the squeaky wheel that gets the oil"? Applied to the human resources development (HRD) function, it means that usually the persons most likely to get a course added to the curriculum are those who are the most vocal, insistent, or senior. But was there a real need for the course? Was the potential for payback great enough to justify the expense? Or was the party requesting the new course responding to a whim or personal bias? In short, did the projected benefits exceed the estimated costs of the program?

Questions like these have prompted training managers to do a feasibility analysis before investing precious time and money in the purchase or development of a training program that has been requested. In addition to the title of the course, here are the major questions you might want answered by the person who is requesting a new course (often called the sponsor, client, or champion):

1. Who is requesting the training (name, title, department)?
2. Why (what need or opportunity exists)?
3. What is the population of trainees (job titles, how many people)?
4. What is the life cycle (before it becomes dated or everyone has been trained)?

5. What will be the turnover and growth (in the jobs noted in no. 3)?
6. How long is training likely to take (course length in hours or days)?
7. What are the topics and course content?
8. What improvements and outcomes are desired from the trainee (estimate the dollar value)?
9. What improvements and outcomes will result for the organization (estimate the dollar value)?
10. Are there any other training objectives (besides those noted in nos. 8 and 9)?
11. Is such training already available (publicly or in other companies; who or where)?
12. What are the factors helping and hindering performance in the workplace?
13. Who has the expertise (subject matter experts to help with no. 7)?
14. Who pays (from whose budget—the requester, trainees, or HRD)?

Evaluating the Request for Training

The answers to these 14 questions have given you a lot of information. Now what will you do with it? You'll prepare an estimate of the costs and the benefits of adding the requested course to your present calendar of course offerings. Numbers 2 through 6 and 11 should enable you to come up with a crude estimate of the costs, while numbers 8 through 10 and 12 should help identify the benefits.

The dilemma: The easier it is to quantify the performance output of a group of employees, the easier it is to demonstrate the impact of training in a cost-benefit analysis. Examples include teller training, driver safety, data entry and retrieval, selling skills, quality improvement, machine repair, assembly, and a variety of production jobs. Yet these are the very jobs where the need for training is not being questioned, and the cost of it is seen as a cost of doing business. Rather, it is in the "softer" areas of training that course justification (before) and vindication (after) are most needed, and most difficult. Let's tackle a few examples.

On the following page are listed titles of four training programs that might be viewed as soft skills areas. Your job is to list two or three benefits that can be converted to dollars that can be saved or generated as a result of the training. Try to avoid benefits that are harder to quantify and convert to dollar values (for example, better motivation, improved climate, happier customers).

Project Management:

Customer Service Skills (by phone or face to face):

Counseling the Problem Employee (a course for supervisors):

Business Writing Skills (letters, memos, reports, proposals):

If you had trouble anticipating the benefits on any of the four courses, look over the list that follows. Of course, the dollar value of any benefit can be appreciated best by knowing what costs the organization was incurring before the course was launched—information that you should have access to in your organization.

Project Management:

◆ Money saved by avoiding time or budget overruns
◆ Elimination of penalty charges on time overruns (on some contracts)
◆ Reduced lost time in renegotiating goals and activities
◆ Resources available as needed (no delays)
◆ Reduced turnover of project team members due to frustration.

Customer Service Skills:

◆ Higher retention of customers, fewer lost
◆ Reduced time spent handling complaints
◆ More new customers as word gets around
◆ Fewer adjusters and supervisors needed on staff over time
◆ More sales per customer for repeat shoppers.

Counseling the Problem Employee:

- ◆ Better retention, lower turnover
- ◆ Reduced costs of recruiting and training replacements
- ◆ Improved productivity as the problem is solved
- ◆ Reduced lawsuits, legal fees, court action
- ◆ Better teamwork and productivity from fellow employees.

Business Writing Skills:

- ◆ Shorter, clearer letters (less time, paper, message units)
- ◆ Reduced need to rewrite to clarify
- ◆ Less time needed by readers who understood initially
- ◆ Fewer mistakes, missed meetings, poor decisions
- ◆ Better proposals resulting in more sales.

When estimating the likely costs and the value of the potential benefits of a training program that does not yet exist, the estimates should be prepared jointly by a training manager and the person requesting the training. Costs are more likely to be known by the trainer, while benefits and their dollar values are more familiar to the client. Moreover, it is primarily the client's responsibility to see that the course, once launched, begins to yield a return on investment. Clients are more likely to take this responsibility seriously if they made the initial estimates of the dollar value of the return over the full payback period.

The Pros and Cons of Feasibility Analysis

Preparing a feasibility analysis takes time and patience—yours and your client's. When managers come to you with a request for a new course, they are not likely to accept with joy the fact that you now want them to work with you in answering 14 questions. Their response is predictable: "I've told you that my people need training. Do you doubt my word?" If you have a training advisory committee, then one of their functions should be to review the requests for training and determine priorities. This can be your reply to the reaction quoted above; the request can't be considered until the committee has this information.

The following list should be of use in preparing you to deal with possible objections to doing a feasibility analysis. Forewarned is forearmed.

SUPPORTING REASONS	INTERFERING REASONS
◆ Better commitment from managers and the people they send to courses (trainees). They are responsible for follow-up and not just for filling seats. ◆ Better performance by HRD staff in containing costs and maximizing benefits. They become performance managers and not just instructors. ◆ Responsibility for success of course back on the job is accepted by graduates and their managers ◆ If the demand for launching new courses exceeds the supply (your time and resources), you now can get managers to justify their requests (or drop them). ◆ Course objectives and content are kept lean, relevant, and behavioral, with focus on performance rather than on the acquisition of information. ◆ HRD can make decisions on the basis of supportive data (what courses to run, to drop, to refuse; what budget is needed—make vs. buy).	◆ We're trainers, not accountants. We lack the needed skills and the time to do preanalysis and postanalysis. ◆ The cost side is hard data, but the benefits are soft and often difficult to quantify and convert to dollars. ◆ We'll continue to run most of our courses, even if costs exceed benefits. So why bother? We're not a cost-profit center. ◆ We have enough trouble getting managers to send people to training without imposing additional constraints or requirements on them. ◆ The outcomes could be damaging to morale of HRD staff and to budget support from top management. We're better off not knowing. ◆ Costs are known up front (before), but benefits may accrue slowly over a long time following the course (after). At what point do you attempt to measure impact?
IN SUMMARY	**IN SUMMARY**
The transfer from workshop to workplace is much greater. By affixing the responsibility for success where it belongs, we've demonstrated that HRD is not an act of faith. Training doesn't cost; it pays!	The potential payback isn't worth the very real effort. Converting estimates and wishes into dollars doesn't make the data any less soft. So why bother? Let well enough alone.

If the Course Already Exists

Suppose you receive a request for a course that already exists, perhaps as a packaged training program that you can purchase or as a public offering that your employees can attend. You now want to find out if the course objectives and performance outcomes of the existing program will meet the training needs of your potential participants. You want to know the feasibility of using a ready-made course. Will it be relevant? Conducted at an appropriate level (not too advanced or elementary)? Timely?

Instructors must make sure that the employees who enroll in their courses know in advance what the course is all about: objectives, prerequisites, expectations, and timing. It can easily cost more than $1,000 for participants to fly back across the country to their own offices upon learning on the first day of class that they've enrolled in the wrong course. One of the criteria in the instructors' evaluations done by the manager is their ability to ensure "the right faces in the right places at the right times." Major providers of instructional skills face the same challenge: to ensure that the trainers who attend their workshops, both public and in-company, are there for the right reasons and are at a level of development where they can benefit from enrolling.

On the pages that follow you'll find an example of a preworkshop questionnaire for a train-the-trainer course that participants complete and return one to two weeks before a workshop. The information gathered from it enables the instructor to identify and contact misfits; to see which participants should be put in pairs on group exercises; and to make slight changes to the workshop content so as to best meet the needs of the participants. Think of this questionnaire not as a form that you might use, but rather as a format that you might copy to create a precourse registration form for your own training program(s)—one that will enable you to qualify your participants in advance, and also help them to determine the feasibility of attending.

INSTRUCTIONAL SKILLS PREWORKSHOP QUESTIONNAIRE

Name: _____

Department/Location: _____

Organization: _____

1. What course(s) are you responsible for? (Give title, length, frequency of offerings.)

   (a)

   (b)

   (c)

2. Are you responsible for teaching, developing materials, enrolling participants, handling the scheduling and facilities arrangements? (Circle the ones that apply.)

3. How many hours of instruction have you delivered personally on the course(s) listed in no. 1 above?

4. How many hours of instruction have you designed (prepared, written, developed materials for) on the course(s) listed in no. 1 above?

5. When and how did you become a trainer? What were you doing before then (in your last assignment)?

6. What are some of your reasons for attending our forthcoming workshop on instructional skills?

7. What do you see as the major distinction between training and education?

8. Applying this distinction to the course(s) you listed in no. 1 above, what percent of your content would you categorize as education and what percent as training? (Your two percentages should add up to 100% on each course.)

	% Education	% Training
(a)	_____	_____
(b)	_____	_____
(c)	_____	_____

9. During our workshop, we'll be going through an exercise that focuses on one class session from the course you listed in no. 1(a). Please select a lesson or class session of one to three hours for your focus. State the topic and the learning objective(s) of the segment you selected:

    Topic: _____

    Objective(s):

10. How many students (average class size) attend this course? ____ Describe or draw the seating arrangement for the session whose objective(s) you recorded above:

11. How is the effectiveness of your course evaluated?

12. What do students say about it? What do they like most and least?

13. What do you like most and least about being an instructor?

Situational Report

One of the challenging (or is it frustrating?) aspects of being an instructor is that from time to time we face unusual situations that come up in connection with the courses we're responsible for.

Think back over the past few months and recall a situation you experienced that stands out in your mind as unusual (perhaps because it was especially exciting, frustrating, rewarding, embarrassing, or whatever). Describe the situation in several paragraphs below, indicating the background, the action that took place, and the results. Also, if there was a moral or lesson to be learned from this situation, state it.

Our Objective and Your Needs

Listed below are 20 of our learning objectives. Your job is to indicate in column A the relative importance or interest of each to you, using a five-point scale with 5 standing for "very important" and 1 meaning "no importance or interest." Do not attempt to have a normal distribution. Your ratings could be all fives, ones, or any combination. Ignore columns B and C.

After this workshop you will be able to

	A	B	C

1. employ the appropriate tools and techniques of needs analysis to determine the needs of learners, before and during a course

2. state the objectives of any training session in a way that satisfies six criteria of a complete behavioral objective

3. establish the entering behavior of learners: their experience, knowledge, attitudes, skills, and expectations relating to the course

4. break down information (stimulus, or S), with responses (R) and feedback (F) after each S, thereby forming a chain of SRF links

5. prepare a behavioral analysis of any task or procedure, identifying the needed knowledge-attitudes-skills

6. select methods and media appropriate to each of the five stages of an instructional system, from preparation to maintenance

7. describe the benefits and limitations of at least five input and five output instructional methods

8. write course materials (handouts, notebooks, learning exercises) in a clear, crisp, interesting manner

9. create visual aids (transparencies, flipcharts, slides) with effective graphics, color, organization, and flow

10. describe and apply at least 10 techniques for getting a high level of participation from all learners and not just the verbal few

11. phrase questions effectively so as to get all learners responding and to elicit relevant responses that show application and not just acquisition of knowledge

12. use discussion leadership skills effectively (summary statements, probes, and other directive and nondirective techniques)

13. deal effectively with different types of problem participants to maintain a positive climate and meet the learning objectives

14. analyze your instructional style and its appropriateness to type of student, subject matter, teaching method, and personality

15. teach inductively (lecture) and deductively (Socratic), indicating when and how to use each method

16. identify at least eight workplace factors that jeopardize transfer of training and describe how to deal with each

17. carry out a cost-benefit analysis that can be used to evaluate feasibility (before design) and impact (after training)

18. strengthen transfer of training from class to workplace, using at least five of the 20 techniques taught

19. evaluate instruction against 10 questions (criteria) that establish the course's effectiveness at four levels

20. prepare the person(s) responsible for delivering training and maintaining performance (instructors, supervisors, team members).

CHAPTER 3

THE SYSTEMS MODEL FOR TRAINING

Upon completing this chapter you should be able to

◆ list the five components of a system, illustrating each with a training course

◆ illustrate the three subsystems of training

◆ estimate the percentage of time currently spent on each of these systems

◆ indicate what time allocation changes should produce better training results

◆ explain why evaluation must be done before and after training

◆ select from case studies the one(s) to be modeled in your training programs.

Every student of management is familiar with systems. Managers must plan, schedule, direct, and control a variety of activities—research and development, manufacturing, sales, distribution, maintenance, training. They rely on systems to do this. We might define *system* as a group of interrelated components working together to produce a desired result or predetermined goal. There are five components to any system: goal, input, process, output, and feedback.

Let's take a familiar example: a heating system. It was designed to keep the building's temperature within a certain range. That's the goal. The input includes fuel, air, and ignition. The process is combustion. The output is heat (BTUs), distributed by conduction, convection, or radiation. The feedback (control) is provided by a thermostat that is constantly evaluating (monitoring) the performance of the system, telling the furnace when to go on and off (input) and, in a commercial heating system, modifying the process as well, so as to get the best combustion. Let's look at the systems model, this time applied to training.

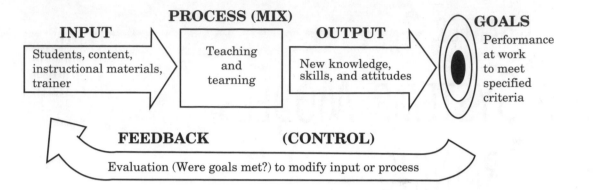

In a training system, the goal is performance in the workplace, to meet predetermined standards or expectations. The input includes students, course materials, instructor(s), facilities, and audiovisual equipment. The process is called learning, facilitated by teaching. The output is new knowledge, attitudes, and skills as outlined in the learning objectives. And feedback comes from the evaluation tools and techniques used to monitor and improve performance. Without a thermostat, your heating system isn't a system at all, and the temperature will be out of control. Without evaluation tools and techniques, your training system isn't a training system at all, for you lack the means of monitoring and ensuring that the desired performance criteria are being met.

The Subsystems of Training

Training can be viewed as three distinct systems: evaluation, instruction, and maintenance. These systems describe the events that occur before, during, and after the learning process. Three separate and distinct activities make up each of the three systems, as noted below:

The Evaluation System. Before designing or delivering instruction, trainers must evaluate three things (a process often referred to as needs assessment or performance analysis):

◆ the entering behavior of the trainees (knowledge, attitudes, and skills [KAS])

◆ the terminal behavior of trainees (desired performance at work)

◆ the work environment (factors that help or hinder performance on the job).

The Instruction System. The design and delivery of a training program typically follows a three-stage learning model, as illustrated and outlined below:

- ◆ acquisition (trainee must acquire new KAS)
- ◆ demonstration (examples, cases, and models bring KAS to life)
- ◆ application (trainee must practice new KAS with hands-on activities).

The Maintenance System. After trainees have completed a course, three things must be maintained to ensure full return on the training investment:

- ◆ performance on the job (must be inspected, recognized, and reinforced)
- ◆ course itself (must be refined, revised, and kept current with needs)
- ◆ evaluation measures (data needed to maintain performance and course).

Stages in the Training Process

The five stages of training are defined on the chart that follows, which illustrates the typical goals, content, and methods of each stage.

Stages in the Training Process

	PURPOSE OR GOAL
Stage One: **PREPARATION** in which we prepare both ourselves and the trainee for each task at hand	We must first prepare ourselves: Have we established the trainee's entering behavior and the desired terminal behavior? Do we have the needed materials at hand? Is the location for training ready? Is it free of interruptions? Have we allotted enough time? Then we must prepare the trainee by explaining the terminal behavior in a way that will create a desire to learn, establish rapport, and begin the instruction on an interactive, trainee-centered basis.
Stage Two: **ACQUISITION** in which we tell the trainee the new information that is needed to perform	We must impart the knowledge, attitudes, and skills that the trainee needs. We must define new concepts and terms, and relate them to what the trainee already knows (as established in stage one).
Stage Three: **DEMONSTRATION** in which we show the trainee how to apply what we've just taught	We must demonstrate how the trainee is to apply what we have just taught in stage two. Our purpose is to clarify and bring to life new knowledge by providing examples: ◆ "model" examples that show ideal, correct behavior that the trainee can imitate ◆ typical real-world examples that show correct and incorrect behavior for the trainee to discriminate between.
Stage Four: **APPLICATION** in which we give the trainee hands-on practice in applying the things taught in stages two and three	We must provide the trainee with the opportunity to practice and to experience the consequences of correct and incorrect performance. Our purpose is: (a) to get feedback that tells us what the trainee does and does not understand; (b) to build correct patterns, or habits, and thus improve the trainee's retention (and transfer of training back on the job); and (c) to develop the trainee's self-confidence.
Stage Five: **MAINTENANCE** in which we check out and reinforce the performance of trainee back on the job	We must inspect what we expect, giving and getting feedback on how well our training objectives (terminal behaviors) were met. Our purpose is: (a) to measure the effectiveness of our training, and improve future efforts accordingly; (b) to get return on our investment (better transfer of training); and (c) to show the trainee that correct performance is important and that we do care.

CONTENT	METHODS AND TECHNIQUES
We find out what the trainee already knows, so we know were to begin. We learn what interests or hobbies the trainee has (so that we can pick analogies and examples that will relate to the trainee's frame of reference). We tell the trainee what he or she will be able to do at the end of the training session, and why it is important.	Ask questions, use survey research (for larger group of trainees), get a brief autobiographical sheet from each trainee listing related knowledge, skills, training, education, and experience. Give trainee a brief outline of the topics to be covered (and possibly a training schedule—dates, topics, places). Often is it appropriate to have the trainee briefly observe employees at work, doing the things that the trainee is about to learn.
We introduce the trainee to the subject matter or course content: facts, concepts, principles, policy, procedures, techniques, values and beliefs. In short, our content consists of knowledge, attitudes, and skills (KAS).	This stage is usually handled by lecture for groups, or one-on-one instruction for individuals. Sometimes training texts (manuals, handouts, workbooks) also are used. Sometimes the material can be taught through self-study (programmed instruction).
We provide concrete, specific examples (cases, incidents, situations) that illustrate the stage two content (KAS) being applied at work. Sometimes the examples show model or ideal behavior; sometimes they show correct and incorrect behavior (see comments to the left).	Demonstration can be done by the instructor or by having the trainee observe an employee at work. Demonstration can be real world or staged. Demonstration can be done live or presented through audiovisuals (film, videotape, audiotape, slides), in which case there is greater stimulus control (we know in advance how it will go).
We give the trainee problems to be solved, tasks to be performed, procedures to be followed, forms to be completed. Our role has now shifted from teacher to observer: We are diagnosing the trainee's need for further instruction or practice.	In teaching manual skills, the trainee can be given real tasks or simulations (in which we have greater stimulus control). In teaching cognitive or verbal skills, we often simulate the real world, using case study, role playing, in-basket exercises, or other techniques that give the trainee an opportunity to apply the concepts and skills that were just acquired.
We observe the trainee on the job, giving praise for correct behaviors and constructive criticism for incorrect ones. If we are not the trainee's immediate supervisor, then we should find out how well this person is filling the role of coach during those important first few days or weeks on the job. If necessary, we should prepare the supervisor for his or her role in maintaining the trainee's new behaviors.	Use check lists, observer rating sheets, "shopping" surveys, and whatever other forms or techniques will help to standardize the quality of the observations made of the trainee's performance on the job. Find out where the trainee felt most and least comfortable during the first few days on the job, and how the training of future trainees can be improved.

Some Questions for Your Consideration

1. In a survey of more than 200 instructors conducted by a provider of instructional skills workshops, respondents indicated by percentages how their time is allocated over the three systems just discussed. Their responses typically fell into the ranges shown below:

   Evaluation System   15-20%
   Instruction System   75-80%
   Maintenance System   0-5%
                        100%

   What would you estimate your own percentages to be in each of these three areas of activity? Is this the most appropriate allocation of your time? What would the ideal percentages be, given the status of your course(s) and the nature of your trainees and their work environment?

2. In the course(s) you are responsible for teaching or designing, what methods and media do you make frequent use of in each of the three stages of the learning model: acquisition, demonstration, and application?

3. Looking at the three activities that make up the Evaluation System, how would you score yourself on each (use a scale of one to 10)? What actions do you feel are called for to improve your course's effectiveness during evaluation?

4. Looking at the three activities that make up the Maintenance System, how would you score yourself on each? Again, what actions do you feel are called for to improve your course's effectiveness during maintenance?

5. Looking at the three stages of instruction, what percentage of time during the course is devoted to acquisition? To demonstration? To application? Do you feel this allocation is appropriate, or are you "robbing Peter to pay Paul"?

Evaluation: Before or After Training?

Were you surprised to see that evaluation was the first of the three subsystems? To be sure, most trainers also want to evaluate impact after their courses are over. But they can do so only if they have first identified their trainee's entering behavior, the desired levels of a trainee's terminal behavior, and the workplace conditions that help or hinder graduates as they attempt to apply what they acquired. The remainder of this chapter contains three case studies that document the impact of training with hard data:

Measurement of organizational productivity. Any organization has systems in place for tracking against productivity goals and standards: unit costs, quality controls, reject and scrap rates, time required to process, sales quotas, customer satisfaction, and so on. Whenever training is aimed at improving productivity, it is relatively easy to measure its impact by comparing the performance data collected before training with posttraining data. This was done at Binney & Smith with dramatic results.

On-the-job training vs. formal classes. Two matched groups of 20 newly hired employees at Johns Manville received training on the operation of a plastic pipe extruder. In one group, employees were trained on the job, while the other group received instructions in class. Formal (structured) training proved to be superior in that it took less time to reach mastery, performance levels were higher (better output, reduced scrap), and employees were better able to deal with production problems that came up.

Measurement of action plan implementation. The Coca-Cola Bottling Company of San Antonio ran 64 supervisors through eight sessions of supervisory training. After each session, participants prepared an action plan that outlined specific steps to be taken back on the job as a means of applying their new concepts and skills. The cumulative benefits obtained through the implementation of these action plans totaled $526,000 more than the cost of the course—a 15-fold return on investment!

Measurement of Organizational Productivity

Binney & Smith, an Easton, Pennsylvania, manufacturer of art and craft supplies, ran their middle management and first-line supervisors through a 10-session supervisory training program. The aim: greater involvement of employees in work group meetings, resulting in improved productivity and better job satisfaction.

Classes met once a week over three months. Each session began with a videotape or film that introduced the concepts and skills associated with the topic of the day: goal setting, problem solving, planning and scheduling, counseling, and decision making. This was followed by case studies, role plays, self-assessments, scripts for analysis, games, and simulations. At the end of the session, each participant developed an action plan that outlined what actions would be taken back on the job. This was reviewed with the participant's manager and implementation was begun. Progress was reported at the next class. The first session was used to assess competence. The last session repeated the assessment as a measure of improved competence, and also got participants to report the results of their action plan implementations. Four measures were taken to evaluate the program's effectiveness:

◆ **Competency improvement.** The *Managerial Assessment of Proficiency MAP* was used to measure 12 competencies. Preassessment to postassessment gain was 54% on the eight competencies that were taught and 3% on the competencies not taught.

◆ **Participant evaluations.** End-of-course evaluation sheets showed a gain of 59% from "value expected at start of course" to "value at end of course." (Raw scores on a 10-point scale went from 4.4 to 7.0.)

◆ **Action plan follow-up.** Several months after the course, participants were contacted individually to see the results of implementing the action plans they generated in class. Two examples stand out. (1) A corporate distribution manager initiated regular work group meetings (five to six employees and their supervisor) to solve problems, resulting in a 5% increase in productivity in inventory storage and retrieval. (2) A facility manager gave workers authority (including the halting of production when a problem is recognized) that enabled his plant to reduce scrap costs by more than $100,000.

◆ **Corporate scorecard.** Small-group productivity meetings grew from 31 to 60 per month. Attainment of production quotas now run at 100% or better. Scrap and rework has been reduced by 48%. Quality measures on finished goods now run at 98%.

Senior management expressed high satisfaction with the effectiveness of the training program. Increased output, lower production costs, better quality, and a positive work climate on the plant floor all point to an ROI in the six months following training that is five to six times the cost of the training program. Still greater returns lie ahead. As a result of the program, Binney & Smith has begun the process of transcending management-employee communication barriers that had been in place for years. By moving from a parental, autocratic style of management to a team-focused, participative style, the company is repositioning itself for new growth and development.

On-the-Job Training vs. Formal Classes

Johns Manville,* a manufacturer of building materials, undertook a 14-month study in which employees assigned to operate the Rainville plastic

*A detailed report on the Johns Manville study may be found in two issues of the *Training and Development Journal:* "Training: What's It Worth?" 1976, 30:17, and "Cost-Effectiveness: A Model for Assessing the Training Investment." 1978, 32:27.

extruder (which converts raw material into plastic pipe) were divided into two groups of 20 trainees each. One group received training on the job; the other group was instructed in class. The groups were matched according to age, education level, community background, and test scores of aptitude.

Five measures were taken as a means of evaluating the relative effectiveness of the two training modes: quantity, quality, worker competence, cost effectiveness, and worker attitudes. Here are the criteria:

◆ **Quantity:** measured by count and weight.

◆ **Quality:** based on visual and dimensional criteria, using a test device.

◆ **Worker competence:** concealed closed-circuit TV monitored the ability to set up production, turn out quality pipe, and recover from two production problems (machine variables that were introduced remotely).

◆ **Cost effectiveness:** actual expenditures were tracked on materials and labor, including the instructor's hourly rate.

◆ **Worker attitudes:** an attitude inventory was developed to assess the perceptions of trainees toward their training and the job.

The results of the study showed significant benefits of formal classes over on-the-job training (OJT) on three of the five criteria. The formal classes required 72% less time than OJT and resulted in a higher level of competence. Production losses (waste) were 70% less than they were for OJT. The most dramatic result was a 130% success rate for production problem trouble shooting after formal training as opposed to OJT. There was no significant difference in attitude, and the cost of training was only a dollar different between the two groups. In one sense, the cost variable is not a fair comparison, since formal classes would be used to train many more than 20 workers over time, and the cost per trainee would continue to drop as the (fixed) developmental costs are written off.

Measurement of Action Plan Implementation

The Coca-Cola Bottling Company of San Antonio installed an eight-session course on supervisory skills. Sixty-four first-line supervisors went through the course in four groups of 16 participants. Sessions were instructed by department heads and senior management, with a different team of two managers teaching each session. These managers had previously attended an intensive six-day program to prepare them for their instructor role. Class meetings were held two weeks apart so that participants could meet with their managers following each class. At these meetings the participants spelled out the actions they planned to take to put into practice the concepts and skills acquired in class. The managers then had to approve, modify, or reject each action plan.

The action plans, an integral part of the course design, fixed responsibility with each participant to translate their new learning into specific actions in the workplace. Action plans can thus be viewed as a means of putting management by objectives into operation among first-level supervisors, whose typical day is activity oriented rather than goal oriented. Here are the parts to the four-page action plan completed by each participant after each of the eight training sessions:

◆ Subject: the specific area(s) you have picked for improvement

◆ Objective: what is to be accomplished—the purpose of the plan

◆ Goals: the specific targets by which you will measure progress

◆ Problems: the barriers that might hinder you in carrying out your plan

◆ Solutions: how you plan to avoid or deal with the problems

◆ Resources: what people, time, or equipment you need to carry out the plan

◆ Activities and time: what steps (actions), sequence, and time are needed

◆ Costs: what the overall cost of implementing your plan will be

◆ Benefits: what benefits you expect and their estimated dollar value

◆ Commitment: when you and your manager will next review progress.

Three months after the class was over, participants came together again for an executive briefing at which supervisors took 10 to 15 minutes each to report to their peers and upper management on the results of their follow-through on the action plans. More than half of them reported financial data: costs and benefits of implementing their action plans (savings, increased sales, reduced waste, shorter collection times, less absenteeism). Their costs-benefit figures were tallied at the end of the briefing. The results were impressive. The company realized an ROI of $526,000 over and above the cost of running the training program.

CHAPTER 4

TWO TYPES OF TRAINING OBJECTIVES

Upon completing this chapter you should be able to

◆ distinguish between mediating and terminal behavior; give examples of each

◆ give examples of verbs that are and aren't acceptable in a training objective

◆ describe the three parts to a complete training objective

◆ indicate different wording for conceptual and procedural training objectives

◆ prepare or edit training objectives to meet six criteria.

On our systems model of training, the output consisted of new knowledge, attitudes, and skills (KAS). These are known as learning objectives and can be evaluated during a workshop and immediately at the end of it. But does the learner's attainment of new KAS in class mean that the goal of improved performance in the workplace will be met? Not necessarily, since many factors besides training influence one's behavior on the job.

This distinction between workshop and workplace performance is extremely important to trainers as is evidenced by the variety of terms we use to describe the two sets of behavior (in much the same way that Eskimos have 22 words to describe snow—it's such an important part of their lives). Some of the terms you may encounter in the literature of training are shown in the chart on the next page. The terms we'll be using most often are *mediating* and *terminal*.

WORKSHOP	WORKPLACE
learning objectives, enabling objectives	job standards, appraisal criteria
knowledge-attitudes-skills	performance indicators
mediating behavior	terminal behavior
formative behavior	summative behavior
comprehension and acquisition	retention and application

Let's take an example of each type of behavior, drawn from a course to train bank tellers in how to cash checks. Notice that the verb is the key indicator of whether an objective is to be met in class or on the job. (Ask yourself whether the verb describes behavior that occurs in the workshop or in the workplace.)

Workshop objective: a mediating behavior. The teller will be able to distinguish between "on us" and "on other bank" checks; will describe the five conditions of negotiability (acceptability); and will indicate whether a given check is or isn't negotiable (can be cashed or deposited).

Workplace objective: a terminal behavior. Given a check to be cashed or deposited, the teller will determine whether the transaction can be completed or not (based on its negotiability and whether the account or the presenter is with our bank). The error rate must not exceed 1% (that is, at least 99 of every 100 checks must be processed correctly).

Preparing Course Objectives

Robert Mager's book, *Preparing Instructional Objectives,* set the guidelines for specifying the desired outcomes of a course. The key word in a learning objective is the verb. It must describe a behavior that the learner performs after instruction. This verb must also be observable and measurable. Consider two examples (the first does not qualify; the second does):

◆ Upon completing the course, the learner will be able to appreciate the value of new customers, understand the importance of spelling their names correctly on the account information card, and treat them with respect.

◆ Upon completing the course, the learner will be able to cite the average annual dollar volume of a new customer, verify the spelling of their name on the account information card, and use their name twice while welcoming them and thanking them for opening an account with us.

Directions: Indicate by check mark whether each of these statements is a behavioral objective. They are taken from a course that teaches the principles of flight to persons qualifying for their private pilot's license.

Upon completion of this lesson, the student pilot will be able to

	YES	NO
a. completely understand the aerodynamic properties of airfoils	___	___
b. write, in his or her own words, the definition of an airfoil	___	___
c. state the physical law by which an airfoil produces lift	___	___
d. be motivated to a degree that is enough for the student pilot to be able to know the meaning of "chord line"	___	___
e. list the four forces that act on a plane in straight and level flight	___	___
f. really understand Bernoulli's Principle and apply it to an aircraft's wing	___	___
g. discriminate between statements that are true or false concerning "angle of attack" and "angle of incidence"	___	___
h. select, from a given list of aircraft parts, those that are considered airfoils	___	___
i. fully appreciate and grasp the significance of the ability of a plane to fly	___	___
j. understand and enjoy the experience of small-aircraft flying	___	___
k. spell correctly the words *aerodynamics, Bernoulli, incidence, stratosphere,* and *vacuum.*	___	___

You may want to compare your evaluations with our evaluations of the objectives for the principles of flight course:

a. No. The verb "to understand" cannot be observed or measured.

b. Yes. Of course, we'd prefer to see the criteria of acceptability stated.

c. Yes.

d. No. We're not measuring motivation. "Define chord line" would be a Yes.

e. Yes.

f. No. The word "really" cannot strengthen the problem verb "to understand."

g. Yes. Simpler wording: "Define angle of attack and angle of incidence."

h. Yes.

i. No. We cannot observe or measure "appreciation" or "grasping."

j. No. We cannot observe or measure "understanding" or "enjoyment."

k. Yes. Probably the easiest to observe and measure, although it has nothing to do with flying a plane. So let's add another criterion: Course objectives should be observable, measurable, and relevant.

Parts of a Behavioral Objective

Training objectives should always be stated in terms that are observable and measurable. For example, suppose we are teaching someone to type, and set one of our objectives as follows: "Trainee must be able to type rapidly and with accuracy." This is a poor objective as it stands. What does "rapidly" mean? What is "accuracy"? A better training objective is this: "Trainee must be able to type at least 40 words per minute (average of 10 minutes), and must have no more than three corrections per 200 words." This objective is observable and measurable.

When we are preparing objectives for courses that are concerned primarily with the teaching of procedures or techniques, our behavioral objectives should contain three elements:

◆ the condition (event, situation) that the trainee must respond to

◆ the behavior (response) we want the learner to make

◆ the criteria of acceptability for evaluating the learner's behavior.

Let's look at an example of an objective taken from a course designed to train retail sales clerks. This particular lesson deals with handling money and making change. The three parts of an objective are labeled beside it:

Condition (S) Given a customer paying for merchandise with paper money whose face value exceeds the price,

Behavior (R) sales clerk will follow the correct procedure (five steps) for making change,

Criteria (F) with no more than two omissions over six transactions (that is, two out of 30 steps is our "tolerance").

In learning theory, the smallest unit of behavior is the stimulus-response-feedback unit (SRF). A learning sequence consists of a chain of SRF links. If we now look again at the sample objective, we see that the condition is the stimulus—the event or situation that stimulates the learner to respond. The behavior is the response we want the trainee to make. And the criteria enable the trainee and instructor to have feedback on how well the learning is progressing. (Notice the letters *S, R,* and *F* in front of the three parts of the sample objective.)

The objective we just examined is mainly concerned with the sales clerk's skill in following procedures correctly. Trainers sometimes prefer objectives that focus on knowledge rather than skill. Here's an example of the same objective, rewritten to stress knowledge:

Condition (S)   Upon completing the lesson dealing with handling money and making change,

Behavior (R)   the sales clerk will be able to list the five steps to be followed when a customer needs change,

Criteria (F)   giving them in correct sequence and stating why each is important to the accuracy of the transaction.

Incidentally, the five steps referred to in both of our sample objectives are:

1. Acknowledge the size of the bill(s): "That's $3.95 out of $20."
2. Place bill on ledge of register until transaction is complete; don't put it in drawer.
3. Select change from drawer, working from smallest size up; give it in same sequence.
4. Count change on to counter or into customer's hand; state when to do each.
5. Thank customer for shopping here; place bill in register.

In our two examples of training for retail sales clerks on how to make change, one objective began by describing a specific condition or stimulus: "Given a customer paying...." The other objective simply named the lesson but did not describe a condition or stimulus: "Upon completing the lesson dealing with...." Why the two different formats?

When your course objectives deal with the learning of facts, rules, and concepts that are nonprocedural in nature (the sequence of their presentation is not important, and the learner's ability to perform in the workplace is not dependent on a particular initiating condition or stimulus), it is appropriate to identify the course (lesson, module) and not to attempt to describe the initiating condition. When your course objectives deal with the learning of actions that are procedural in nature and performed in response to a specific condition, your course objective should begin with a statement describing the condition so that the trainee learns to associate the desired behavior with that condition. The principles of flight objectives that you evaluated earlier were conceptual rather than procedural. Therefore, all of them followed the general statement: "Upon completion of this lesson, the student pilot will be able to...."

In contrast, consider a course on selling skills and the lesson on how to deal with common types of objections. Here the conditions or stimuli are quite specific:

- ◆ "Given a customer who says, 'Your price is too high,' the salesperson will...."
- ◆ "Given a 'Let me think about it' customer, the salesperson will...."
- ◆ "Given a 'We don't need it' response, the salesperson will...."

Suppose the course on selling skills contains 10 common types of objections. Rather than have 10 separate course objectives, they might be expressed as one objective: "Given a list of 10 common types of customer objections or 'put-offs,' the salesperson will be able to state the appropriate response to at least eight of the 10." Notice that this objective states a criterion that allows for performance that is less than perfect. You saw this earlier in the retail sales example of how to make change "with no more than two omissions over six transactions (that is, two out of 30 steps is our 'tolerance')." Whether or not a performance objective should allow tolerance in its description of the criteria usually depends on how critical or essential the desired performance is.

Mediating vs. Terminal Behavior

In preparing objectives, we must distinguish between mediating behavior (which occurs in class) and terminal behavior (which can occur in class as well as on the job). The verb is the key to whether an objective is mediating or terminal. Here are two lists of behaviors that illustrate the difference:

MEDIATING BEHAVIOR	TERMINAL BEHAVIOR
Trainee must be able to name the three parts of a standard automobile jack and describe where the jack should be placed to raise a flat tire off the ground.	Trainee must be able to assemble the jack, place it correctly on the automobile, and operate it so as to raise a flat tire off the ground.
Bank teller must be able to state the five things to look for in cashing a check (negotiability factors), and to describe the procedure for dealing with problems on each factor.	Bank teller must be able to process a mixed batch of checks that contain errors, handling at least 18 of the 20 correctly, (that is, cashing or refusing them correctly).
Secretary will be able to identify dependent and independent clauses, words used in apposition, words in series, and conjunctions used to separate two clauses or sentences.	Secretary will be able to transcribe dictation, inserting commas where needed (to separate clauses, appositives, words in series, two clauses or sentences).

Mediating behaviors usually contain verbs like *state, name, describe, identify, explain, show, define,* and *give an example.* These behaviors occur in a class but not in the real world. (For example, no manager ever went up to a secretary and said, "Identify the dependent clauses and the appositives in this paragraph." But the terminal behavior is quite common: "Marge, you forgot to put commas in this letter in two places—here, and here."

Terminal behaviors usually contain verbs that are observable: *assemble, conduct, perform, produce, process, fill out, compute,* and *arrange.* These are the behaviors we want of the learner in the real world.

The question arises: Why have mediating behaviors at all? Don't we always want to state our objectives in a way that reflects what the learner does in the real world? Perhaps we do. It is not always possible, however, to measure or observe our trainees under the actual conditions for which we are training them. Suppose we are developing a course to train nurses how to evacuate the hospital and move patients in the event of fire. We could develop a simulation, of course. But it would cost time and money, and would not be able to induce the element of panic and fear. So we might settle for mediating behavior instead: "Describe the process for evacuating a ward, noting the five steps to be taken and three precautions to be observed." The training of firefighters, police cadets, airline pilots, military personnel, and nuclear power plant supervisors involves the development of many behaviors that can be simulated but never duplicated. In such cases, trainers may have to accept the trainees' verbal descriptions (mediating behaviors) of their real-world performance in situations that, it is hoped, will never occur.

How Do These Objectives Rate?

Listed on the next page are sample learning objectives from four different courses. Your job is to evaluate each against the six criteria listed below, entering your evaluations in the last column. Then use a separate piece of paper to rewrite objectives or portions of them, as required.

1. Is it appropriately mediating or terminal?
2. Are the initiating conditions (stimulus) specified?
3. Are the criteria (response acceptability) spelled out?
4. Is it a relevant (useful) objective?
5. Is it behavioral (measurable)?
6. Is it sufficiently discrete (small, workable)?

COURSE	OBJECTIVE	EVALUATION
Printing Process (trade school)	Upon completing the lesson on engraving, the apprentice printers will be able to give the three names for the process (intaglio, gravure, engraving), describe the steps in making a plate (both by acid and mechanically), and list at least three types of printing jobs in which engraving is used commercially on long press runs.	
Letter Writing	Given a customer complaint letter to be answered, the branch manager will be able to (a) identify the purpose of the reply, (b) select the most appropriate style and format for the reply, and (c) describe some of the things to be included in the letter (apology, restatement of problem, statement of empathy, corrective action taken).	
Structural Steel Framing (a design course)	Given a blueprint showing the elevations (cutaway) of six different nuclear boiler installations, the designer will be able to specify the appropriate cross-bracing (system design and size and type of structural members) in at least five of the six installations.	
Management Development	Upon completing the session on motivation, the participants will be able to distinguish between Herzberg's "motivators" and "hygiene factors," indicating which is intrinsic and which extrinsic, and giving at least four examples of each that are operating in the participant's work group (section, department).	

You may want to compare your evaluations with our evaluations of the four learning objectives listed in the preceding chart. First of all, notice that the middle two describe actions to be taken in response to specific conditions, or stimuli. Therefore, the wording starts with "Given a...." In contrast, the first and last objectives are from courses that seem to be academic: Learners must "name, describe, list, distinguish between, give examples." These verbs describe mediating (classroom) behavior. Therefore, the wording starts with "Upon completing the lesson (session)...."

In short, the initial wording of all four objectives is appropriate. When we look at the verbs describing the desired performance, however, they describe mediating behavior in all four examples. This is appropriate in the last example, since much of management development is educational rather than training in nature (knowledge rather than skills). But the other three examples might have the learner perform rather than describe performance. More specifically, would it be appropriate for the apprentice printers to prepare an engraving plate and pull a proof? In the course on letter writing, having the learner (branch manager) draft a reply letter is the terminal behavior we want, and there is no reason why we can't get that behavior in class. As for the structural steel framing course, we need to know if the verb "to specify" is what our learner does at work, or whether the learner must add the cross-bracing to the blueprint. Does "to specify" describe a mediating or a terminal behavior? If mediating, can we redraft the objective to state the terminal behavior?

All four objectives state the criteria, or conditions of acceptability: at least three types of engraved printing jobs; at least four things to be included in an apology letter; at least five of the six nuclear boiler installations; at least four examples of "motivators" and of "hygiene factors."

CHAPTER 5

ORGANIZING THE LESSON PLAN BY OBJECTIVES

Upon completing this chapter you should be able to

◆ list the four things a good lesson plan (course outline) will contain

◆ describe two formats for preparing a lesson plan

◆ indicate the advantage of each format

◆ select the format better suited to your own training and state why

◆ describe how handouts and visuals can be incorporated into a lesson plan.

The behavioral objectives of a training program enable us to evaluate the program's effectiveness by finding out how well the trainees can perform the behaviors outlined in the objectives. This is why well-written course objectives will include the criteria of acceptability: "The trainee will be able to give at least four reasons why…."; "The trainee will be able to name the eight parts of an area gantry robot and describe the function of each."

Behavioral objectives serve another purpose. They enable us to evaluate the appropriateness of the course content, and this, in turn, influences the selection of methods and media. The relationship is illustrated below:

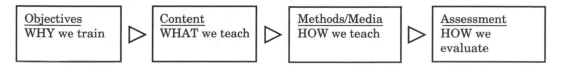

| Objectives WHY we train | ▷ | Content WHAT we teach | ▷ | Methods/Media HOW we teach | ▷ | Assessment HOW we evaluate |

A good course outline will contain these four elements. The appropriateness of each can be evaluated against the prior elements driving it. That is, what we teach must be appropriate to why we train, and our methods and media must be appropriate to our content and objectives. In the Instructional Design Checklist contained in chapter 24, you'll find criteria for evaluating the appropriateness of each of these elements.

The pages that follow contain two useful formats for a lesson outline. In the first example, a four-column format enables the course designer or instructor to display entries side by side under the four headings, thus preserving the dependency relationship. In the second example, these same four headings are listed down the page, giving the designer or instructor more space per objective. The elements are interdependent, of course, and a good outline will show the relationship of each to the others. The first example can accommodate a number of course objectives on the same page. In contrast, the second example requires a separate page for each course objective (desired behavior).

Study the two forms. Then answer the questions at the end of the chapter. This exercise should enable you to select the form best suited to your needs, and use it in your future course designs. Do your own lesson plans follow a standard format? Should they? Is the behavioral objective always shown along with the content, methods, and media?

Course Design Blueprints: Two Outline Formats

The final stage of course design is the creation of an outline that serves as a blueprint for the construction (development) of the course. The writer(s) who will develop the learning exercises must know four things that a good course outline will contain:

Desired behavior: course objectives—performance expected of the learners, in class (mediating behavior) and in the workplace (terminal behavior)

Subject matter: course content—the knowledge, attitudes, and skills that must be taught in order to produce the desired behavior

Methods and media: instructional tools and techniques to be used to impart the subject matter (lecture, video, lab, role plays)

Criterion tests: learner responses to be elicited by the instructor as feedback needed to monitor and evaluate progress.

The degree of detail that a course designer provides depends on the writer's familiarity with the objectives, content, and methods and media (in much the same way that an architect may provide a more detailed blueprint to a new contractor than would be needed by an experienced contractor, or one who had worked closely with the architect on past projects).

BEHAVIORAL OBJECTIVES What the learners will be able to do after the course.	SUBJECT MATTER (COURSE CONTENT) What you will tell or show the learner; the information learners need to meet the objectives.	METHODS AND MEDIA How you plan to get the message across.	TESTING (RESPONSES) How you will know the objectives have been met.

HUMAN RESOURCES DEVELOPMENT	TOPIC:		TIME (est.):
	AUTHOR:	SOURCES:	
	UNIT NO.:		

OBJECTIVE (Upon completing this topic, the trainee will be able to):

SUBJECT MATTER (Course content to be taught in order to produce the terminal behavior outlined above):

METHODS, MEDIA, TECHNIQUES, INSTRUCTIONAL STRATEGIES:

CRITERION TEST (How will you know that trainee has met the objective?):

Integrating the Lesson Plan, Handouts, and Transparencies

One way to organize a course is to have each lesson plan on file in a three-ring binder, following by the transparencies (or black-and-white copies of them) and the handouts. Such a binder is valuable to many persons. Present and future instructors need a copy, since it represents the complete documentation and set of materials needed to teach the course. Training managers and course counselors or enrollers need a copy so as to answer questions relating to objectives and content. Supervisors considering a course for members of their work group can get a quick overview and make informed decisions on enrollments.

The lesson plan should be cross-referenced to the visuals (slides, flipchart exercises, transparencies) and to the handouts (readings assignments, tests). Copies of these visuals and handouts should be included in the binder immediately behind the lesson plan that serves as their cover sheet.

Some Questions for Your Consideration

1. What are some of the advantages of the first (four-column) outline format on page 45? Of the second example (one objective per page)?

2. Would you see any benefit in using both? Or would you only use one? Why?

3. Which do you prefer? Why?

4. Imagine a training department in which every course had been filed in a three-ring binder containing a detailed outline (on one of these two formats). What are some of the uses and benefits you can see for this type of course documentation?

CHAPTER 6

TRANSFER OF TRAINING

Upon completing this chapter you should be able to

◆ identify and give examples of three sets of factors that influence transfer

◆ indicate which factor the instructor has most and least influence over

◆ describe three types of retention curves following training; give examples

◆ select three or four of 20 ways to improve transfer in your training programs

◆ identify factors (from 50) causing low transfer in your training programs.

Training is an investment. If the learners apply back at work what they acquired during their learning, there will be a return on the investment. If they do not, then the training time was merely spent (and hence wasted) rather than invested. Why would learners not apply at work what they were taught during their training? Three sets of factors are operating and serving to help or hinder the transfer of learning from class to job: personal, instructional, and organizational. Let's look at some examples of each.

Personal factors. These include such things as motivation (Does learner want to be in class? Know it already, or believe so? Enjoy the work and the job?); ability (Does learner have the ability to learn?); attention (Can learner concentrate? Or are weightier matters interfering—sickness, a marriage breaking up?); and relevance (Does learner see the course as relevant to the job and to personal needs?).

Instructional factors. These include such things as course design (appropriateness of methods and media; facilities and equipment; length and objectives); emphasis (theory vs. practice; knowledge vs. skills; talking vs. doing); instructor (credibility; effectiveness); follow-up (Do trainers get feedback on learners' performance after training? Are actions taken accordingly, on the trainee and on the course design?).

Organizational factors. These include such things as climate (Do the norms, culture, and expectations of fellow employees and managers support the new behaviors that were just learned?); time and timing (Does trainee have time to do things the way they were taught? Was opportunity to apply new learning fairly immediate or too delayed?); degree of fit (Do local procedures, forms, equipment agree with those taught to the learner?).

The first of these three factors is internal to the learner, and there is often little the instructor can do to influence the personal side other than attempt to screen the participants (by assessing their entering behavior prior to the course and then making every attempt to get the right faces in the right places at the right times). The second and third factors are external to the learner. Instructors, course designers, and management share a responsibility for establishing a maintenance system that will recognize and reinforce the desired behavior of learners as they attempt to apply at work what they learned in class. On the pages that follow, you will find 20 ideas (actions, techniques) that address the organizational factors noted above.

Learning Curves

Introductory psychology texts typically contain a chapter or so on learning and remembering. Learning can be plotted as a curve to show how the learner's performance improves over time (the length of a course). Such a curve is shown below, superimposed on the learning model.

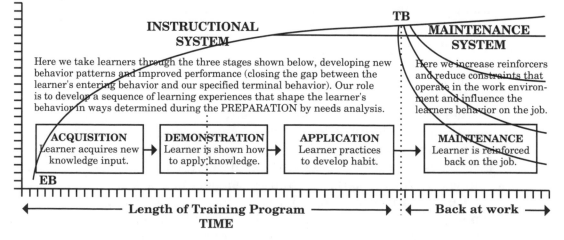

Following a course or learning program, the newly acquired knowledge, attitudes, and skills will transfer in one of three ways, as indicated in the retention curves shown above. The reasons for each are described on the next page.

Continued improvement (curve still climbing). When skills can be immediately applied and improved through use, performance continues to grow. Some examples are typing, computer data entry, foreign language, supervisors conducting future performance appraisals, salespersons on each new presentation.

Stable performance (curve levels off). Some types of behavior are binary—learners can do it or they can't, and it's not a matter of degree. Examples are remembering a concept or theory; spelling a name correctly; recalling a policy; citing a source; performing an operation (for example, calculating a square root); recalling a formula (for example, converting centigrade to fahrenheit).

Declining performance (curve shows rapid decay). When new learning is not applied, or when attempts to apply it are met with negative consequences ("Look, I don't care what they told you in class, you're working for me now. Here's how I want it done."), trainees will revert to old habits, wrong behavior, or withdrawal (nonresponse to situations they've been trained to respond to).

Trainers have a major responsibility to do whatever they can to keep the retention curve as high as possible (to ensure maximum transfer from workshop to workplace). In contrast, educators focus their concern on the learning curve and getting it as high as possible. Once the course is over and the final grade is determined, however, their responsibility ends.

Twenty Ways to Improve Transfer and Maintenance

As you read the ideas that follow, place a check mark in the box in front of each one that is worth considering for the course(s) you teach. These are the ideas you will want to discuss with your manager or a fellow instructor who shares responsibility for the course. Most of the items will not apply, or will take more time than you have to make them work. If you end up implementing three or four of these ideas, the ROI will be well worth it.

❑ 1. Each participant completes an action plan that spells out what steps will be taken back on the job to apply the newly learned concepts and skills. Participant discusses this with supervisor, and both agree on when and how the plan will be implemented. Copy is filed with the instructor for follow-up.

❑ 2. Schedule an alumni(ae) day about five to eight weeks after the course, as a time when your participants come back together to report (10 to 15 minutes each) on the things they have accomplished by putting to use the concepts and skills they learned in the class. Make this day your "graduation." Invite their supervisors.

❑ 3. Where you are teaching the entire job to a new hire, have each trainee develop a job description as an ongoing part of the course. Each new procedure or responsibility that you teach gets summarized on the job description in the trainee's own words. This then becomes a "transmittal document" that goes with the trainee to the supervisor.

❑ 4. Create an association of those who have completed the course who meet once a month for their continued growth and development. They have a program committee to identify areas of interest for further training; you assist by getting speakers or instructors, from within or outside the organization.

❑ 5. Develop a newsletter that serves to maintain and reward good performance through recognition: interviews with graduates, success stories, instructive articles, contests (quizzes, case studies for analysis, "what would you have done?").

❑ 6. Require each learner to send in a critical incident report that summarizes a problem encountered back on the job, and that describes how the tools and techniques acquired during the course helped the learner to tackle the problem and resolve it. Make successes public in newsletter or house organ.

❑ 7. In jobs where it is appropriate (customer contact jobs, for example), conduct a shopping survey by phone or in person to see how the graduate is able to handle a number of problems and questions that the shopper poses. Then give immediate feedback and reward, based on performance.

❑ 8. Instead of running courses intensively over a short time span, stretch them out and run them extensively, interspersing classroom time with time back on the job. This gives participants time to apply and act on each new set of skills, meet with their supervisors, and address any differences between class and job.

❑ 9. Bring the managers (supervisors) of your participants together before the course starts (and, if appropriate, after it is over) to brief them on the objectives, content, format, and most important, on their role as a partner with you in the training of their people. Spell out their responsibilities; give them a letter of agreement.

❑ 10. In situations where people work in pairs or teams (data processing clerks, secretary and boss, customer service representatives), schedule them to attend training in pairs. Develop your training exercises in a way that strengthens their responsibility to support one another.

❑ 11. Use needs analysis techniques and instruments that can be repeated at some interval after the course to generate data to be fed back to the graduate and the boss (climate survey, supervisory style inventory, communication style assessment). Get the two parties together to interpret the change.

❑ 12. Make use of planning sheets, flowcharts, checklists, and other job aids in the training program, so that trainees can take these back to the workplace and use them on the job. Conduct an audit of the workplace to see how well these job aids are being used; reward and reinforce this behavior.

❑ **13.** Set up an assessment lab or a series of modular (independent) self-assessment exercises, and schedule each graduate to come in "for a free, no-obligation checkup." Give the graduate feedback on strengths and weaknesses, and discuss where they have been able and unable to apply what they learned.

❑ **14.** Work with department heads or division managers to select a training coordinator for each major unit of the organization. Work with these people in scheduling follow-up activity to help participants as they leave training and go back on the job. Equip these coordinators with checklists or job aids.

❑ **15.** Form a training advisory committee consisting of key managers from the major divisions and departments of your organization. Use this group for input (guidance) in developing your courses, and for output (follow-up) in monitoring and reinforcing good performance by graduates.

❑ **16.** Give participants surveys and assessments that they can go through and have their manager, subordinates, customers, or users go through, so that you are influencing the immediate environment of your participant.

❑ **17.** Provide participants and their managers with a list of behaviors to be observed and evaluated back at work following training. Request a copy of this checklist to be returned to the instructor within 30 days of the end of course.

❑ **18.** Create a performance contract in which participants agree to meet the criteria spelled out in the contract in exchange for training. Participants evaluate themselves against these criteria and notify the training department of fulfillment.

❑ **19.** Run training programs for natural work groups (by department, branch, location) rather than for a mixture that runs across organizational lines. Address specific needs of each homogeneous group rather than conducting "one size fits all" courses for a widely heterogeneous audience.

❑ **20.** In jobs where productivity can be measured (number of sales made, transactions processed, trucks loaded), schedule a contest for the period immediately following training. Set up a reward schedule so as to have many winners among your graduates.

Transfer of Learning from Class to Job

Instruction is effective only to the degree that new learning is converted into performance back at work. This process is known as **transfer.** Many factors influence the degree of transfer and determine the return on the training investment. The pages that follow contain a checklist of 50 factors that influence transfer of training. They are grouped under five major headings:

Course design

Instructor's skills and values

Trainees' abilities and perceptions

Workplace environment

Role of managers and supervisors

The checklist is designed to enable you to evaluate a specific course and the degree to which transfer of training is likely to take place. You might use it in planning a new course or evaluating an existing one. On each of the 50 factors, your job is to circle the rating that best describes the course.

2   Strong; no problem with this factor.

1   Moderate; this factor is present, but needs improvement.

0   Weak or absent; this factor is negligible or nonexistent.

Let's take an example to illustrate:

A.   To what degree does trainee's supervisor know what was taught and seek ways to reinforce new behavior on the job? ... 2 1 0

In this example, suppose the supervisors of your trainees have themselves been through the course or a briefing before you launched the course for their people. They are very supportive and encourage their people to apply the things they learned in class. Thus, you would circle the 2.

Now suppose that the supervisors believe in training but are not very well acquainted with the course and what their people are learning to do. They give general encouragement but cannot be as specific in their feedback and reinforcement as they should. You would circle the 1.

Now suppose that the supervisors were too busy to concern themselves with the course and the things their people learned from it. They spend little if any time recognizing and reinforcing new behavior when their people come back from a course. You would circle the 0.

Course Design

1. How relevant is the content to the trainee's needs? 2 1 0

2. How appropriate are the instructional methods and media? 2 1 0

3. Are there enough job aids, checklists, references for use on the job? 2 1 0

4. How effective are the learning facilities and equipment? 2 1 0

5. How well do the trainees like the course design? 2 1 0

6. Is the length of the course appropriate to its objectives? 2 1 0

7. Do trainees have enough time in class to practice and refine new skills? 2 1 0

8. How smooth is the flow and transition from one session (topic, lesson) to the next? 2 1 0

9. Do trainees get enough feedback to help them check progress and make corrections? 2 1 0

10. What kind of image does the course have throughout the organization? 2 1 0

Total of the 10 numbers circled above

Instructor's Skills and Values

11. How well does instructor know the subject and the work environment of the trainees? 2 1 0

12. To what degree does instructor use language, examples, and analogies that the trainees can relate to? 2 1 0

13. Does instructor spend additional time when trainees are having trouble learning? 2 1 0

14. To what degree did instructor teach deductively (Socratic method and not inductive lecture method)? 2 1 0

15. How effective is instructor's skill in keeping class interactive and well paced? 2 1 0

16. Does instructor have the respect of management and the trainees' supervisors? 2 1 0

17. To what degree does instructor have learners doing things rather than talking about how to do them? 2 1 0

18. How well do trainees like the instructor as a person? 2 1 0

19. Does instructor follow up after course to see where trainees can or cannot apply what they learned? 2 1 0

20. To what degree does instructor prepare trainees to deal with barriers (problems, frustrations) they face back at work? 2 1 0

Total of the 10 numbers circled above

Trainees' Abilities and Perceptions

21. How favorable is the trainee's attitude toward the course and the work it prepares one for? 2 1 0

22. To what degree do the trainees possess the necessary prerequisites (entering behavior)? 2 1 0

23. Are members of the trainee's work group practicing the skills and concepts being taught? 2 1 0

24. How free are trainees of personal handicaps or problems that disrupt their concentration on the course? 2 1 0

25. To what degree do trainees see themselves rather than the instructor as responsible for their learning? 2 1 0

26. How stable is the trainee's job status and personal status (marital, health)? 2 1 0

27. How clear is trainee on how the course will be teaching new ways of doing things? 2 1 0

28. How committed are trainees to learning and applying new ways of doing things? 2 1 0

29. Do trainees have the abilities (courage, insight, verbal skills) to stop the instructor when they don't understand? 2 1 0

30. How does trainee perceive the rewards (benefits) of applying the new learning back on the job? 2 1 0

Total of the 10 numbers circled above

Workplace Environment

31. How well do the workplace norms (expectations, culture, climate) support the new behavior? 2 1 0

32. To what degree did the timing of the training agree with the opportunity to apply it at work? . . . 2 1 0

33. Do the physical conditions in the workplace support the desired behavior? 2 1 0

34. How readily does the course content translate into appropriate behavior on the job? 2 1 0

35. How permanent and resistant to change are the policies, procedures, equipment? 2 1 0

36. To what degree do peers and other employees support the trainee's new behavior at work? . . . 2 1 0

37. How frequently do the trainees get to apply on the job what they learned during training? 2 1 0

38. To what degree do trainees receive frequent and specific feedback in the weeks following training? 2 1 0

39. How well understood are the rewards and penalties associated with performance? 2 1 0

40. To what degree does the course have the respect of the trainees' peers and supervisors? 2 1 0

Total of the 10 numbers circled above

Role of Managers and Supervisors

41. How strongly do managers and supervisors believe in the course and those who give it? 2 1 0

42. To what degree do supervisors want their trainees doing things the way they learned in class? 2 1 0

43. Do supervisors explain the value of the course before their trainees attend? 2 1 0

44. To what degree are supervisors rewarded by their managers for coaching? 2 1 0

45. Are assignments made so as to give trainees immediate opportunities to apply their new learning? 2 1 0

46. To what degree do supervisors send trainees to the right courses at the best time, based on need? . . . 2 1 0

47. Are supervisors taking time to recognize and reinforce the trainees' new behaviors back on the job? 2 1 0

48. To what degree are the supervisors good role models, practicing what is taught in the course? 2 1 0

49. How well do supervisors understand the objectives and content of the course? 2 1 0

50. To what degree do supervisors have a development plan for each subordinate that includes training? 2 1 0

Total of the 10 numbers circled above ☐

Total of the five boxes (out of a possible 100) . . . . ☐

CHAPTER 7

ESTABLISHING PERFORMANCE INDICATORS

Upon completing this chapter you should be able to

◆ explain what is wrong with "rapidly" or "courteously" as objectives criteria

◆ describe the importance of performance indicators in eight HR functions

◆ define and illustrate two types of job functions: caretaking and risk taking

◆ explain how goals and standards relate to these two functions

◆ give at least three subcategories of knowledge, attitudes, and skills (KAS)

◆ illustrate the EB-TB gap on a specific behavior for a writing skills course

◆ generate standards for at least three duties on a job description

◆ identify the abilities relevant to your job (from list of 30 competencies).

A common weakness of training objectives is their failure to pinpoint the specific behavioral expectations with measurable performance indicators. For example, a course for administrative assistants includes an objective that states that the learner "will be able to type letters, memos, and reports rapidly and accurately." But what do these two adjectives mean? A better wording that defines *rapidly* might be this: "will be able to type at least 60 words per minute (average), after corrections." Similarly, we might define *accurately* as "with no more than two errors per 100 words (average)."

Let's take another example, this time from a soft skills course: customer courtesy for bank tellers. Upon completing the teller training course, the learner "will be able to treat all customers with courtesy." If we were visiting branches of the bank and evaluating the effectiveness of the course, what behavior would we look for? If a teller was not discourteous or rude, would they get credit for customer courtesy? Or are there positive behaviors that go with courtesy? If so, these should be indicated: greet customer; use customer's name, wish customer a nice day; excuse yourself from window when checking the customer's balance; offer to give customer the current balance listed on the account.

In this chapter you'll meet many examples that illustrate how our expectations of performance can be spelled out in very specific terms. After examining a model showing the central role of performance indicators in all the functions of human resources management, you'll see how behavioral expectations apply to two different kinds of jobs: caretakers (routine) and risk takers (one-time goals). Thereafter, you'll see three examples of performance indicators:

- ◆ a behavioral analysis showing desired knowledge, attitudes, and skills required of persons who write business letters, memos, and reports

- ◆ a job description that illustrates the process of identifying the standard; (expectations) for each duty or responsibility

- ◆ 30 competencies associated with the role of an instructor, so that jobholders can evaluate the relevance and their proficiency on each.

Performance Indicators: The Heart of Human Resources Management

Manpower, methods, machines, materials, money. These are the resources needed to run an organization. Any organization. When managers purchase methods (systems), machines, materials, and money, they typically take time to spell out the criteria and expectations (performance indicators) that must be met. These indicators then serve as the basis for selection, modification, maintenance, and full utilization of the resource. In short, managers need performance indicators as the basis for managing their resources.

Yet when we are faced with decisions affecting the human resource (manpower, that fifth M), all too little attention is given to spelling out in detail the criteria and expectations (performance indicators) to be met. No wonder managers are uncomfortable when conducting selection interviews, performance appraisals, training sessions, counseling and career planning, and disciplinary action—all the managerial responsibilities relating to the performance of people at work. And that's a big chunk of a manager's job!

A SYSTEMS VIEW OF
HUMAN RESOURCES MANAGEMENT

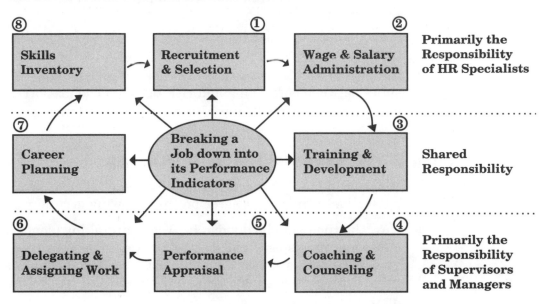

As shown in the above model, the process of breaking a job down into its components (expected outcomes, or performance indicators) is central to all the responsibilities and actions that go with the effective management of employees. This process is the shared responsibility of three parties: the jobholder, the supervisor or manager, and the HR specialist (usually a consultant or personnel department staff member). In jobs where many employees fill the same position and perform similar work, a task force can be created to generate performance indicators.

Two Types of Jobs

Some jobs are stable: The duties and responsibilities remain relatively constant from year to year (bank tellers, machine operators, drivers, customer service representatives, word processors). The performance indicators for such jobs should be useful over time. Moreover, they should be useful from one organization to another. (How different are the duties and responsibilities of one bank's tellers from another's?) Such employees are hired **to fill** jobs and to meet predetermined performance indicators. In contrast, consider the fact that 25% of all present-day jobs didn't exist 10 years ago! One characteristic of our sociotechnical age is that many employees are hired **to create** jobs for which predetermined performance indicators do not exist (project managers, researchers, new business ventures, jobs changed by technology). Here the duties and responsibilities must be regularly renegotiated. We might label these two types of work as caretaker (filling duties) and risk taker (creating duties). Or as stewardship and entrepreneurship. Or as regular work and stretch work. Whatever labels we attach, the following points are worth noting:

♦ Most employees have both types of work present in their jobs.

♦ Job descriptions outline the caretaking duties and responsibilities of a job.

♦ Management-by-objective statements (goals and objectives for next year) outline the risk-taking expectations of a job.

♦ Employees and their supervisors should agree on how the job splits between caretaking and risk taking. (The proportion might be 0-100, 50-50, 100-0, or anything between.)

Using Performance Indicators To Manage

If employees and their supervisors are to manage their time and their resources effectively, they must agree on the following ground rules:

♦ How the time is to be divided between caretaking (sometimes viewed as time spent) and risk taking (often seen as time invested). Both are necessary in most jobs. The mix varies over time. Both parties should regularly review and renegotiate the mix.

♦ What performance indicators will be applied to the caretaker side of the job (standards, quotas, conditions).

♦ What performance indicators will be applied to the risk-taker side of the job (goals, objectives, expectations).

♦ How the various people management functions of supervision (selection, training, appraisal, career pathing) will be administered on the basis of these performance indicators.

Notice that we have not mentioned wage and salary administration in our list of people management functions. In most organizations, payroll decisions are made on the basis of many factors besides an individual's performance. There is agreement on the value of having performance indicators for the other supervisory functions, but managerial support might be jeopardized altogether if each employee's pay were to be tied directly and entirely to a well-defined set of performance criteria. Some organizations have set up different systems of compensation to accommodate for the two types of jobs. Caretaker work is rewarded by raises that move a person through the salary range for the job, from minimum through midpoint up to maximum. Risk-taker work is rewarded by bonuses, incentives, and money set aside (budgeted in an escrow account) and released in amounts contingent on the level of performance. At present, the greatest value of performance indicators is to jobholders and their managers (nos. 3 through 7 on our systems model), and of lesser value in the functions managed by the personnel department (nos. 1, 2, and 8). But this will change over time.

Trainers require performance indicators to evaluate the impact of courses on the subsequent behavior of participants back on the job. The process of generating performance indicators should also be part of courses that teach supervisors how to conduct selection interviews, give on-the-job training, counsel employees, and conduct performance appraisals.

How To Generate Performance Indicators

The five steps outlined below are generally carried out by two parties (or a task force on which both parties are represented): the person(s) holding the job and the supervisor(s) of the job. A personnel or training specialist may also accelerate the process and provide consistency of results throughout the organization.

1. The two parties should agree on what portion of the job is caretaker and risk taker (filling duties and creating new outcomes, regular and stretch work). This can be expressed as a percentage of work time to be spent on each.

2. The key results areas or major responsibilities should be outlined under each. These are typically in the range of two to six headings in each of the two groups.

3. Under each of these key results headings, both parties should agree on the performance indicators: "How will we track and evaluate performance, and who will make the observations and record the data? In short, how will we keep score so as to play the game better and better?"

4. Since a given job (position description) is usually held by many employees, the results of Step 3 should be reviewed by other jobholders and their supervisors for completeness, fairness, and feasibility. Modifications are incorporated, and the performance indicators are accepted for use by all jobholders, their supervisors, and trainers who teach the job or portions of it. (This last step, modification and acceptance, is much easier when a task force approach is used on Steps 1 through 3.)

5. A performance maintenance schedule is set up to specify different checkpoints or time intervals, for evaluating jobholders on the different performance indicators (in much the same way that the performance maintenance schedule on a car has different intervals for checking the oil, antifreeze, battery, and transmission fluid).

Duties vs. Competencies

On routine jobs that are stable over time (caretaker), the key results areas can be broken down into duties and responsibilities, with performance indicators spelled out for each. Although the process takes time, there is a big return on the investment: Such jobs won't change markedly from year to year, and there are often dozens and maybe hundreds of employees filling a given caretaker job.

In contrast, when we attempt to outline performance indicators for jobs that change from one project (assignment, task force, program) to another, the payback period is shorter. So is the attention span and patience of these more entrepreneurial types (risk takers), whose preference for action over planning is often strong. To be sure, the projects and programs they manage must have the expected outcomes specified and quantified. But such criteria are often expressed as organizational goals rather than as personal yardsticks. In such cases, it may be preferable to use performance indicators based on competencies rather than duties. Competencies are the generic abilities that underlie the specific activities we perform at work. Let's look at some examples of two competencies that are generic to a variety of jobs, such as sales, supervision, scheduling, and customer service.

Time management:

- develops a daily "to do" list, negotiating priorities with stakeholders
- adjusts priorities up or down daily, based on prior goals met and on negotiation
- refuses or avoids non-value-adding work, or sets low priority on it
- assigns and accepts work based on actual cost per hour for self and others
- delegates and develops others to do routine work, reducing own load by 10%
- schedules similar tasks to be done in batches
- increases ratio of time invested to time spent by at least 5% per year
- reduces personal and organizational stress.

Getting unbiased information:

- requests information in a complete, concise, well-organized form
- elicits information with ease, using questions, and probes appropriately
- listens attentively, summarizing and rephrasing to confirm understanding
- recognizes incomplete or inconsistent replies; probes to improve accuracy
- uses questions effectively (directive, nondirective, self-appraisal)
- maintains control of aim, bias, and climate during communications
- processes information, analyzing then synthesizing into more useful form.

Example of a Behavioral Analysis
for a Business Writing Skills Course

	ENTERING BEHAVIOR (Present)	TERMINAL BEHAVIOR (Desired)
KNOWLEDGE (facts, rules, theory, concepts, procedure)	◆ Sentences long and sometimes rambling; writers unaware of this. ◆ Writer makes common use of passive voice ("It was decided that.... It has been brought to our attention that...."); no knowledge of why passive voice is poor writing. ◆ Output has low readability due to many long, imprecise words, such as *facilitate, coordinate, retain, obtain, endeavor* ("Every endeavor will be undertaken to facilitate the successful implementation of your program.").	◆ Sentences should not exceed an average of 17 words; shorter is better. ◆ Convert to active voice ("The team decided that.... We've noticed that...."); passive is used only when subject (person acting) is unknown. ◆ Use at least 75% one-syllable words to give high readability, such as *help, work with, keep, get, try* ("I think we can help to make your rollout a real success.").
ATTITUDES (feelings, values, perceptions, beliefs)	◆ Long sentences and a polysyllabic vocabulary with many unfamiliar words are the mark of an educated writer. ◆ Management will think I haven't thought things through or done my homework if I don't deliver a multipage document. ◆ There's a certain formal style to business writing that I should model: "This department intends to facilitate an increased exchange of information."	◆ Key executives and busy, successful people get a lot of message into a crisp, lean writing style; less is more (readability, attention). ◆ Management has had poor models. Give them a brief document with attachments that provide depth for those who want it. ◆ The formal style of the past is as useless today as powdered wigs. Write the way you speak: "I'd like to see more swapping of ideas...."
SKILLS (manual, cognitive, perceptual—things we do)	◆ There is little or no outlining or planning prior to writing; free flow of thought; not always logical or consecutive. ◆ Writer makes heavy use of business jargon; dull, ponderous, imprecise, or pompous writing; not conversational. ◆ First dozen or so words are often wasted: "I have just received your letter dated March 12, in which you inquire about the availability of our...."	◆ Writer knows before starting that a letter, memo, or report will have five paragraphs or four sections; good organization and flow. ◆ Writer makes use of colorful, interesting, memorable expressive words, analogies, and figures of speech; conversational ◆ Key message is up front, usually in the first paragraph: "Yes, our 1987 model is still available. I'm delighted that you're interested in...."

THE JOB DESCRIPTION

Position title: Supervisor of food service

Reports to: Manager of administrative services

Entry requirements: High school graduate

Definition: Operates the kitchen, cafeteria, and executive dining room front 8:00 a.m. to 3:30 p.m. Provides lunch for 500-800 people daily. Lunch consists of three hot offerings plus sandwiches, soups, salad bar, beverages, and desserts. The cafeteria opens at 8:00 a.m. for continental breakfast. Lunch is served from 11:30 a.m. to 1:30 p.m. in both the cafeteria and the executive dining room. Beverages, snacks, ice cream, and frozen yogurt are available throughout the day, from 8:00 a.m. until 3:30 p.m., when the cafeteria closes.

DUTIES	STANDARDS
1. Oversees the staffing (hiring, training, assigning, appraising), supervising a staff of two cooks, four preparers/servers, two dishwashers, two cafeteria attendants, two waiters or waitresses for the executive dining room, two cashiers, and one assistant supervisor.	1. Prompt filling of vacancies. All to be part time except two cooks, assistant supervisor, and supervisor. No additional positions or people to be added without authorization by manager.
2. Plans the menu on a four-week repeating schedule, ordering all food and supplies, and maintaining sufficient inventories to meet the anticipated head count. Posts menu for the week every Monday.	2. Popularity of offerings to be in response to quarterly survey of employees, with ratings never below 75%. All three hot lunch offerings must be available until at least 1:00 p.m..
3. Maintains high standards of sanitation, cleanliness, and safety, conforming to local and state health authorities and OSHA requirements.	3. No unsatisfactory ratings; kitchen and serving line ready at any time for visit by VIPs or health officers.
4. Caters special functions (employee picnic, community day, open house tours), bringing in part-time help as needed.	4. Special budget and extra help to be approved in advance of all special functions.
5. Approves all invoices from suppliers and sends to purchasing for payment. Maintains records of costs, revenues, waste, and spoilage so as to advise the manager of administrative services on income, costs, and recommended prices.	5. Monthly profit and loss report. No changes in price of cafeteria items without approval by management. Cafeteria to be operated at a break-even pricing of offerings.
6. Maintains tight security and neat storage of all food products and inventory so as to ensure minimum shrinkage through theft or spoilage.	6. Less than 1% shrinkage. Area always locked when unattended (food storage area).

Thirty Instructor Competencies

Listed below are a number of competencies that apply in varying degrees to your role as an instructor. As you read through them, assess first the relevance of each skill to the course(s) you teach. Then assess your proficiency, or level of skill, in each category. Rank yourself accordingly: "extremely, above average, average, below average, or negligible."

1. **Educational psychology.** Ability in understanding and applying the learning process: how behavior is shaped, how people learn, and how knowledge, attitudes, and skills can be imparted and acquired through training.

2. **Task and behavioral analysis.** Ability to break down large, complex concepts and procedures into simpler, manageable tasks, then build them up again in a learning sequence; skills of analysis and synthesis.

3. **Andragogy vs. pedagogy.** Ability to teach in an adult-to-adult manner, using trainees as a resource, rather than functioning in a parent-to-child manner in which trainees are dependent on the instructor and not one another.

4. **Catalyst vs. lecturer.** Ability to function as a catalyst, arranging experiences and facilitating learning rather than being mainly a lecturer and imparter of heavy doses of information.

5. **Audiovisual support.** Ability to select and use audiovisual hardware and software effectively (slides, overhead projector, flipchart, chalkboard, video, computer-assisted instruction, programmed learning).

6. **Inductive and deductive.** Ability to teach inductively (lecture method) and deductively (drawing learning points from students via the Socratic method), using each when appropriate.

7. **SRF links in a chain.** Ability to impart information in an interactive, participative manner, eliciting responses frequently and with ease, so that a learning sequence is a chain of stimulus-response-feedback links.

8. **Principles and examples.** Ability to use analogies, anecdotes, illustrations, cases, and models, both verbal and visual, to bring learning points to life with vivid, relevant, and memorable examples.

9. **Organization and flow.** Ability to organize material into the best sequences (logical, psychological, chronological) from the learner's standpoint of need to know, comprehension, and retention.

10. **Coaching and counseling.** Ability to recognize individual learner needs, values, problems, and to provide individual help as appropriate (counseling, the buddy system of paired trainees, special assignments).

11. **Facilities management.** Ability to check out and set up a learning environment, making appropriate use of facilities and taking care of the physical comfort needs of trainees so as to enhance learning.

12. **Records management.** Ability to maintain records on learner progress and performance, and to keep orderly files of all course materials (exercises, tests, handouts, simulations, outlines, objectives).

13. **Research to keep current.** Ability to accommodate for new needs or opportunities brought up by learners or organizational changes, by researching new information and translating it into classroom materials and exercises.

14. **Organizational awareness.** Ability to interpret and translate the course content into the strategies, norms, structure, culture, power networks (politics), and goals of the organization, so that the course furthers the organization's mission.

15. **Behavioral objectives.** Ability to prepare and communicate the objectives for each segment of a course in clear, behavioral (results-oriented) terms that describe learner outputs in observable, measurable ways.

16. **Computer competence.** Ability to use the computer as a teaching aid or a tool for tracking the progress of learners, either individually or in the aggregate (composite tracking of each group's performance).

17. **Writing skills.** Ability to write course materials, tests, program reports, and proposals in clear complete, crisp, compelling language that produces the desired results in the reader.

18. **Oral presentation skills.** Ability to speak in a way that sustains interest by making good use of vocal dynamics, inflection, articulation, dialect, dialog, colorful language, humor, and body language.

19. **Questioning skills.** Ability to use different types of questions effectively (directive, nondirective, self-appraisal, reflective, rhetorical) to elicit facts and feelings with equal facility.

20. **Criterion testing.** Ability to construct or use criterion tests to track progress against the predetermined mediating (classroom) behaviors, measuring each when appropriate.

21. **Listening and feedback skills.** Ability to listen effectively, analyzing the intent and meaning as well as the words and content of the speaker, then restating and playing back the message to verify understanding.

22. **Delegation skills.** Ability to delegate, assigning task responsibility and authority as appropriate, to learners and to staff support personnel so as to extend one's individual effectiveness.

23. **Time management.** Ability to manage time, make trade-offs, and negotiate with learners so that the needs of the organization and the trainees are both met within the specified time framework of the course.

24. **Charismatic role model.** Ability to provide learners with a role

model that they will respect and want to emulate (to learn from behavior modeling as well as from the instructional process).

25. **Instructional design skills.** Ability to develop course methods, media, and materials according to established principles of instructional systems design, so that the course remains current and delivers a high impact on the learners.

26. **Network of contacts.** Ability to keep contact with (and, when appropriate, make use of) other instructors and resources of the organization (to network so as to leverage one's time and talent, and to keep up to date.

27. **Use of three-stage learning model.** Ability to take learners through all three stages of the learning model of acquisition-demonstration-application (tell-show-do), with every new concept, skill, or procedure that is introduced.

28. **The learning contract.** Ability to set contract with each new learner, establishing their entering behavior (what they already know and feel) and the desired terminal behavior (what they'll be able to do) on completing the course.

29. **Continuity and flow.** Ability to maintain continuity and flow during the course by stating subobjectives, testing for them, making connective statements, and charting progress so that learners have a part-to-whole direction.

30. **Learner centered.** Ability to remain learner centered, sublimating the temptation to meet one's own ego needs to be the expert or the one in charge, and working only to improve the performance of the trainees.

CHAPTER 8

INTERVIEWS AND QUESTIONNAIRES

Upon completing this chapter you should be able to

◆ give at least three advantages and disadvantages of interviews

◆ give at least three advantages and disadvantages of questionnaires

◆ distinguish between directive and nondirective questions; state when used

◆ describe the three-step process in formulating a question

◆ state at least three dos and don'ts in the wording of questions

◆ identify problems in poorly worded questions, and rewrite them.

Whenever you need to get information from jobholders, their supervisors, or customers, the question arises whether you should conduct face-to-face interviews or send out questionnaires. It's not an either-or decision, since each type of survey research has its advantages and limitations. Let's examine some of them.

SURVEY METHOD	ADVANTAGES	DISADVANTAGES
Face-to-face interviews	◆ greater depth of information ◆ able to validate and verify (probe) ◆ easier to get confidential or sensitive information ◆ feelings and attitudes come through	◆ harder to categorize and analyze the data ◆ more time, travel, expense required ◆ limited to fewer respondents; sampling may be necessary
Mailed questionnaires	◆ can be sent to the entire target group ◆ administrative staff can tabulate ◆ all can receive at the same time ◆ no one will feel left out	◆ less depth, more superficial ◆ unable to probe, verify, cross-check ◆ rate of return may be low

Sometimes it's a good idea to prepare the questionnaire and then field test it in a half-dozen face-to-face interviews. Your respondents can help you catch ambiguities, misleading wording, difficult questions, and unclear instructions so that you can revise the instrument before mailing it. In short, you can use interviews to refine the questionnaire. Now let's reverse the order. You can also use the questionnaire to decide whom you should interview. As you study the returns, you'll notice that some respondents gave real thought to their answers and probably have a lot more to say. These are the ones you may want to interview. The key factor in selecting the best survey method is whether you want breadth or depth. Interviews will give you information in depth, but your sample is limited in breadth. Questionnaires will give you breadth of sample, but written replies are limited in depth (and if your questions attempt to get too much information in depth, your percentage of returns will drop off).

Whether you're doing a survey to determine training needs (a needs analysis) or to measure the impact of a training program that has already taken place (an evaluation study), interviews and questionnaires are the two most useful methodologies in your tool kit of data collection techniques. While an individual's responses to your questions often will be subjective or guarded, these shortcomings can be offset by your ability to collect a large quantity of data so that individual differences will "wash out."

The first half of this chapter contains guidelines on how to word questions so as to minimize ambiguity and maximize the probability of getting the kinds of information you are looking for. The second half of the chapter takes you through an exercise in rewriting and editing questions. It should increase your awareness of the many interpretations that are possible from a given wording, and the need to narrow the field of possible responses.

Guidelines for Phrasing Questions

Structure must follow purpose. When we ask a question, we do so to get or give information. Our reason for asking the question will determine how the question should be phrased—whether a highly structured (directive) or a relatively unstructured (nondirective) wording is appropriate. Consider the questions below, taken from a course on time management. The first group illustrates directive questions, while the second group contains examples of the same questions rephrased so as to illustrate the use of nondirective (or, at least, less structured) wording:

Directive questions (highly structured):

(a) Do you think managers have good control of their time?

(b) Is time management more a matter of skill or attitude?

(c) Would a daily "to do" list be of value in managing your time?

(d) Are telephone interruptions a time management barrier?

Nondirective questions (relatively unstructured):

(a) What proportion of management's time do you think is under their control?

(b) What is the role of skill vs. attitude in time management?

(c) What are the pros and cons of keeping a daily "to do" list?

(d) What are some barriers to managing time effectively?

Notice that the first set of questions doesn't contain questions at all. These are statements. They express the instructor's opinion or expectations of a particular answer. The average learner can figure out from the phrasing in the first set of questions that (a) most managers probably don't have very good control of their time; (b) time management must be a matter of attitude as well as skill, or the instructor wouldn't have asked the question; (c) a daily "to do" list is probably a valuable tool; and (d) telephone interruptions must be a major barrier to time management. In short, directive questions require less thought and may, in fact, reveal to the learner what answer the instructor is looking for. As instructors, we often know before we ask a question what kind of answer we're looking for. This "expectation of response" may lead an instructor to structure the question, or stimulus, in such a way as to get the expected answer. It thus becomes a self-fulfilling prophecy in which instructors often fail to find out what the learners really think or feel.

The problem is this: Phrasing a question correctly takes time. The correct wording is not likely to come on the spur of the moment. Often an instructor who has been talking for some time becomes uneasy with this fact and interjects a question to break up the lecture and get some interaction. If the question has not been carefully thought out in advance, however, it will serve no other purpose than that of breaking up the lecture and getting some interaction (which might be accomplished as effectively by having the learners all stand up, stretch, and talk to one another). There's more to asking questions than breaking up a monologue.

Questions that have not been planned in advance are often either too directive (dead giveaways) or too nondirective (unclear, ambiguous). Questions can be finely honed tools for eliciting specific responses and influencing the way people think. Those who earn their living asking questions (selection interviewers, opinion researchers, counselors, consultants) take time to think their questions out in advance, even writing them out in preparation for a session. Instructors can learn from their example, marking up lesson plans and instructor guides by indicating where questions will be posed and by spelling out the specific wording. (In time the process will come more naturally, and writing won't be necessary. But it's a good way to learn the skill of phrasing a question.)

A Three-Step Process

There are three steps an instructor should go through in formulating a question. Although the three occur almost instantaneously in an experienced instructor, an understanding of each step is important in learning how to use questions effectively. They are as follows:

1. **Determine the objective your question is to meet.** Someone has just said or done something (you've just made a point—a learner has just responded—participants are looking confused). You must assess what is going on, what you want to accomplish, and how you can use a question to do it.

2. **Decide what information you want to give or get.** You need to elicit a response (from a particular student or from all of them) that will make a point, confirm understanding, or draw out needed information. What information is required? Should you give it or get it? Inductively or deductively?

3. **Phrase your question so as to accomplish your objective.** You must select words and determine the right amount of structure so that your question is challenging yet answerable. Should it be directive or nondirective? Addressed to the class or to one learner? What alternate wording do you have if your first wording does not succeed?

As in the development of all skills, the phrasing of questions requires practice and critical review. This can be done with the help of a tape recorder, audio or video. Here are two suggestions for improving your questioning techniques:

- ◆ **Script analysis.** Record a segment of one of your classes in which you are leading a discussion or asking questions frequently. Have it typed in script format, with a wide margin for your written comments. Circle each question. Then edit your script, rewording questions that need improvement.

- ◆ **Micro-teaching.** Get two or three trainees or colleagues and teach them a mini-lesson of, say, 10 minutes. Record it. Replay the tape, stopping to discuss each question with your colleagues as they share in your critique.

Dos and Don'ts of Phrasing Questions

The purpose of a question is to elicit a response. In the terminology of learning theory, the question is the stimulus and the answer is the response. The quality of the response you get (clarity, brevity, specificity, appropriateness) is only as good as the quality of the stimulus—the phrasing of the question. Here are dos and don'ts to help you phrase questions effectively:

Keep the wording simple. Don't tax the learner's listening skill with unnecessary words. Here's a complex question that has been edited and redrafted to illustrate our first guidelines:

Instructor: What do you feel are some of the advantages and drawbacks—the benefits and pitfalls, as it were—of having our employees assume the major responsibility for quality control of their own output?

and, after a rewrite:

Instructor: What are the pros and cons of having our employees check the quality of their own work?

Keep the wording neutral. Don't interject your own bias unless you want to make a point. But be careful here: Your learners are quick to recognize bias. Here are two examples of instructor bias:

Instructor: Do you see some real benefits to having employees assume greater responsibility for the quality of their work?

Instructor: Do you think our employees really know how to check effectively on the quality of their own work?

Avoid asking multiple questions that confuse issues. In the example below, the instructor is mixing oranges and apples. One issue is whether employees want more responsibilities, while another concerns who can do the best job of quality control, inspectors or employees. They are independent issues.

Instructor: Do you think employees want to assume greater responsibility, or are we better off having quality control inspectors responsible?

Edit your question for words that can mislead. In the example below, the verb *can happen* suggests negative consequences. The instructor simply wanted to know what the results will be.

Instructor: What can happen when you put employees in charge of checking the quality of their own work?

and, after a rewrite:

Instructor: What are the pros and cons of having employees check the quality of their own work?

Avoid questions that fish for an answer. Don't ask your learners to guess what you are thinking, as this instructor did.

Instructor: Does anyone know of an example that was in the news recently where an organization improved productivity by 17% by having employees do their own quality control checks?

Tell learners when you're looking for a guess. Asking for a guess is a good way to arouse interest or dramatize a point. But let your learners know that you're looking for a guess and that you don't expect them to know the answer. We might take the last example, a poor one showing an instructor "fishing," and reword it to be a good example of asking for a guess:

Instructor: Last week the ABC Co. was in the news for boosting productivity by having employees do their own quality control. Incidentally, what would you guess was the percentage they improved productivity by?

Don't ask questions that are embarrassing or self-incriminating. Your learners will feel uneasy responding to such questions. Here are two examples:

Instructor: Have you ever given quality control responsibility to employees, and then had to reprimand them for errors in the work?

Instructor: Are you doing a really good job of quality control in your group?

Avoid questions that are too simple. No learner wants to look stupid by answering a question that is too obvious or simple. Here's an example:

Instructor: Having each employee responsible for quality control means that they must each check their own work to see that it meets our standards of ... what?

Put the needed information up front. Set the stage. Give the stimulus before you describe the kind of response you want. Our first example violates this guideline. Our second one has been corrected to comply.

Instructor: Can you think of certain things that employees will need help with if they are to be effective in taking greater responsibility for monitoring their own work?

and, after a rewrite:

Instructor: If we want employees to take more responsibility for monitoring their own work, they'll need help in certain things. What are some of these things?

Use specific wording, not general, vague terms. Be as crisp and precise as you can without giving an answer away. General wording will usually elicit general (safe) answers, or no answers. The more specific you can make the question, the more specific the answer can be. Looking again at the two examples of our last guideline, there are three vague phrases that should be translated into more specific wording, as shown below:

"monitoring their own work" → "their own quality control"

"certain things" → "certain tools and techniques"

"need help with" → "need training and coaching in."

The Art of Asking Questions

We ask questions to obtain information. Even before we word the question, we are anticipating a certain kind of answer, and this expectation influences the way in which we phrase the question. Our phrasing, in turn, has a biasing effect on our respondents and the answers they give us. For example, suppose we are preparing to teach a course on time management. We want to find out the needs of our participants in advance, and are preparing a questionnaire. Let's examine some questions and see what information they are likely to yield.

A. Do you feel that you do not manage time as effectively as you should?

Some respondents will answer Yes to mean, "Yes, I do feel that I don't manage time." Others will answer No to mean, "No, I don't manage time." Thus, this wording is poor because it is ambiguous; it mixes a positive ("You do feel …") with a negative ("You don't manage …"). A Yes or a No response can mean the same thing, depending on which part of the question (the positive or the negative) the respondent is answering. Well then, let's reword the question to avoid the mixed positive and negative:

B. Do you manage your time as effectively as you should?

We've avoided the mixed positive and negative, but another barrier remains: The answer is a given. We can predict that the majority of respondents will say, "No, I don't." There's always room for improvement, and the wording of example B merely gets people acknowledging this fact. This barrier (the giveaway answer) will always be present to some degree in questions that call for a Yes or No response. The moral is: Avoid yes-no questions when they don't give you the information you're looking for. Let's try a different wording:

C. How much of your time at work is wasted in a typical week?

Although this wording avoids the yes-no answer, it will elicit many different classes of response, such as "about 12 hours"—"it varies"—"20-30%"—"quite a bit." In this case, data analysis is difficult, if not impossible. The question should indicate what units the answer should be expressed in—hours or percentages.

Another problem with example C is that it introduces strong bias to the answer through the word *wasted*. People do not like to think of their time as wasted. Moreover, there is still ambiguity, for we haven't specified who is wasting their time. If the respondent interprets the question to mean, "How much of your time at work is wasted by others (subordinates, boss, customers)?" then the answer is likely to be high, since most people feel that others are guilty of wasting their time. In contrast, the respondent who interprets the wasting personally is likely to have a much lower estimate. So, back to the task of rewording:

D. What percentage of your time is under your control (that is, you decide what to do)? What percentage is not under your control (someone else—subordinate, boss, customer—determines what you do)? Your two percentages should add up to 100%.

Although this question uses more words than the previous examples, it is much more precise and will yield answers that we can easily analyze. Moreover, the concept of time not under control is more useful than the concept of time wasted, since the word *wasted* implies a value judgment that adds bias.

Let's take a different example. Suppose we want to find out how many of our people are planning their priorities and making up a daily "to do" list. We might start with a question like this:

E. Do you make up a daily "to do" list that establishes priorities for the day?

What's the problem here? For one thing, it's a yes-no question and thus has some bias at work. Most respondents know that they should be making up a daily "to do" list. Thus, many will answer Yes even if they don't do it regularly. Also, a "to do" list may not be interpreted in the same way by all respondents. Many people keep a desk calendar or appointment book, noting meetings and appointments. These people may answer Yes to our question, even though an appointment book is not the same as a "to do" list. So we reword the question as follows:

F. How do you go about planning what you want to accomplish during the day?

This wording avoids the barriers just noted. But it is too unstructured—too open to many answers that reflect different interpretations of the question. Here are some typical answers that illustrate the ambiguity:

◆ "I set goals and then work toward them."
◆ "My secretary keeps an appointment calendar."
◆ "Every night I prepare a 'to do' list for the next day."
◆ "I list what must be done, then assign priorities."
◆ "I think it out while driving to work."

Each of these answers is a legitimate response, indicating the wide range of interpretations that our question might elicit. The problem is not with our wording but with our thinking: We have not thought out what we want to know about our respondent's use of "to do" lists. (We may not even know why we want to know, or what we plan to do with the data. It's always desirable to ask oneself: "What will I do with this data? How will I analyze it? To what will I compare it? What decisions will I make based on the outcome?" Such self-checks will help us word our questions more precisely or eliminate the ones that do not yield information we needed in the first place.)

Let's make some assumptions at this point. Let's assume that (a) our trainees know they should be planning their time better; (b) they do spend some time planning; but (c) they lack discipline in preparing a "to do" list, which usually takes five to 10 minutes per day; and (d) they rarely assign priorities and decide what should be done first, second, etc. To see whether our assumptions are valid, we now can formulate the appropriate questions. Here is an example:

G. In a typical week, how much time do you think you spend listing the work you want to accomplish? When do you usually make up such lists? In the space below, explain how you make use of this list. For example, tell how you decide what should be done first, second, etc.

This wording makes no mention of daily "to do" lists. Those who prepare such lists daily will say so. Those who do not prepare daily lists have not been given any clue that this is the desirable practice. The secret to preparing effective questions lies in not giving the respondent any clues as to what the correct or desired answer might be. People have a tendency to say what they think is expected of them, as revealed by the very wording of the question. Our job, then, is to phrase our questions in as neutral a manner as possible.

Notice that as we progressed through our first set of questions (A to D), and again in our second set (E to G), the wording went from an overly structured (biased, yes-no) form to an overly unstructured form (with a wide range of responses before we thought out precisely what we wanted to know). This is often the case when we formulate questions: Our first attempt is too directive and tells the respondent what we want to hear. Realizing this bias, we tend to reword the question so as to avoid showing our hand. But the result is often too unstructured, as the answers reveal. Only then do we begin to think out precisely what we want to know and how we can get it.

On the next page is a table containing a list of questions designed to elicit the opinions of supervisors toward the company's performance appraisal system. For each question, indicate what barriers, if any, are caused by the present wording. Then give your own rewording of the question.

Exercise in Rewording Questions

QUESTION	PROBLEM	YOUR REWRITE
Do you feel that performance appraisals are a waste of time and there is room for improvement?		
How important is it to prepare a subordinate in advance of the performance review? What should be done? What do you do?		
How much time should be devoted to a really effective performance appraisal?		
Do you feel that annual appraisals are frequent enough? If not, how often do you think they should be held?		
Which of the following do you refer to during a typical performance appraisal? ❏ the job description ❏ record of attendance ❏ last year's appraisal form ❏ the employee's incident file ❏ statements of goals or standards.		
How do you manage to find privacy and avoid interruptions when you conduct a performance review?		
How does your supervisor handle your own appraisal?		

CHAPTER 9

KEY EVALUATION CONCEPTS

Upon completing this chapter you should be able to

◆ explain how the Pygmalion effect relates to personal bias in researchers

◆ distinguish between objective and subjective data

◆ define validity and reliability

◆ illustrate by example two kinds of research: obtrusive and unobtrusive

◆ explain why a researcher must distinguish between needs and wants

◆ give reasons why questionnaires should go to the universe, not a sample

◆ describe the methods used to measure knowledge, attitudes, and skills

◆ list several reinforcers and constraints affecting performance after training.

There are two occasions when a trainer must conduct research to evaluate the behavior of the learners: before training (needs analysis) and after training (to measure impact). This can be done on an individual basis or on the basis of group performance as measured by organizational data such as sales volume, productivity figures, and lost-time accidents. The 10 concepts discussed in this chapter apply equally to data collected before training and after training.

The concept of validity requires some knowledge of statistics when determining whether data really measures what it purports to. If you need to ensure the validity of an evaluation tool or technique, you may want to get help from someone with a statistical background. Of particular use in human resources development (HRD) are calculations of standard deviations and correlation analysis.

One of the major concepts relating to research is the personal bias of the researcher. Few trainers approach an evaluation project with a totally neutral mindset. We typically are doing the research to prove a point:

that there is a need for a training program; that the program did have a significant positive impact; that the instructor was effective in using appropriate methods and techniques. Alas, Pygmalion is alive and well. It's the self-fulfilling prophecy: We get what we expect. Some organizations try to eliminate personal bias by selecting a neutral outsider to do the evaluation research.

Ten Concepts Relating to Needs Assessment

1. **Objective vs. subjective.** Objective information is real, actual, unbiased, impersonal, detached from feelings and personal perceptions. Subjective information is derived from the limitations of the mind of the persons interpreting situations and needs. Facts are objective; opinions are subjective. Objective data is usually more desirable but harder to obtain than subjective data.

   Even when factual (objective) data is available to describe present performance levels, the explanations as to why performance is what it is takes us into the subjective domain. Your respondents are very selective in determining what information to give you and what to withhold, based on their needs, the trust level you establish, their perception of your need, and what they think you want to hear.

2. **Validity and reliability.** The objectivity of the data you receive during a needs assessment can be established by testing its validity (truth or accuracy) and its reliability (repeatability). For example, consider a survey of supervisors that concludes that performance appraisals are unfair because "the personnel department insists on a normal distribution of merit ratings, and all my people are average or above."

   This finding may be reliable; the same finding comes up repeatedly every time you survey supervisors. But it may not be valid. The real (true, valid) reasons why ratings are unfair might be that supervisors have never established gradients or levels of performance; discussed them with subordinates; and agreed upon the behaviors and the criteria that would lead both parties to know what rating is appropriate for an employee's performance on each duty or responsibility.

3. **Obtrusive vs. unobtrusive.** These terms are elegant ways of saying that the person whose behavior you are observing (so as to determine needs) either knows or doesn't know that you are collecting data. For example, suppose we are going to develop a training program for retail sales associates. We might spend a few hours behind the counter with each of a dozen of them, observing their handling of customers, paperwork, and merchandising. This would be obtrusive: They know they are being watched.

   Or, we might hire professionals to do a shopping survey and go through different kinds of transactions (purchases, exchanges, returns) so as to evaluate the skills and needs of the sales associates. This would be unobtrusive. The two problems with obtrusive research are that (a) people are on their best behavior, which elevates performance; and (b) people are nervous, which can reduce performance. Either way, we are not likely to be getting valid or reliable readings.

4. **Survey vs. observations.** Although it's a lot easier to create a questionnaire and send it out to 50 people than it is to go out and observe them or a sample of them, survey research is usually a lot more subjective than observation. People will say what they think you want to hear (which may or may not be what they actually feel). This lowers the validity and reliability of survey data over data collected more directly via observation. Moreover, most organizations have a wealth of data already available in files and computers.

For example, in our earlier example of unfair performance appraisal ratings, one way of testing our thesis that supervisors haven't established performance gradients for each rating level would be to go into the personnel department files and check the comments made by supervisors on the appraisal forms. Did they justify the ratings they gave by pinpointing specific behaviors? Did they describe in specific terms what improvements would be looked for to merit a higher rating next time? Or were the forms filled with generalities and "happy talk"?

5. **Needs vs. wants.** We are simultaneously the beneficiary and the prisoner of our past experience. We know what we know (that's the beneficiary), but we don't know what we don't know (that's the prisoner). Thus, when we ask employees what their training needs are, in one sense we are saying, "Tell me what you don't know that would be helpful to know in your job." And they don't know what they don't know.

For example, the training department of a major firm sent out a survey containing a list of skills needed to be an effective project manager, asking the prospective participants to rank each skill on relevance and proficiency, and then to return the questionnaire. One of the skills was "an ability to use GANTT charts, PERT, and CPM (Critical Path Method)." Respondents ranked this as low on relevance, and they rated themselves average on proficiency. The low relevance scores prompted the trainers to do some follow-up interviews. They discovered that the respondents didn't know what GANTT, PERT, or CPM meant, so they concluded that (a) these things couldn't be too relevant; and (b) they are probably average in proficiency—a safe rating when you don't know what you're talking about!

Moral: When you ask people what they need, they will tell you what they want. It may or may not be what they need. As trainers, we often wear a marketing hat and are obliged to give people what they want. But we also wear the hat of the HRD professional: We'd better also give them what they need to improve their performance.

6. **Sampling vs. the universe.** Whenever we are faced with a sizable population of trainees, this question arises: "Should I involve everyone

in my needs assessment, or can I take a sampling of the universe? And if I sample, how much is enough?" It's easy to send a questionnaire to 200 supervisors (salespersons, project managers). It's almost impossible to interview them or observe them. Here are some of the conditions that might push you toward involving the universe:

◆ The methodology is subjective (questionnaire), so you need more data to add objectivity.

◆ There is benefit to participants in responding, and you don't want anyone to feel left out.

◆ The methodology requires very little time ("Take about five minutes to complete this survey.").

◆ You want people to "buy in" and see the resulting course as theirs and not yours; it's politically better to involve everyone.

◆ The number of returns may be small (for example, 20%), so you want to start with as many as possible.

◆ The universe may be relatively small and manageable to begin with, and shouldn't be further subdivided.

As for the conditions that might push you toward using a sample of the universe, they are just the opposite of the ones listed above, as you will see if you reread the list.

7. **Knowledge, attitudes, and skills (KAS).** Human performance depends upon knowledge, attitudes, and skills—what we know, how we feel, and what aptitudes we possess. In determining training needs, we must assess the types of KAS required to perform effectively.

Knowledge is the easiest to assess. This is usually done via paper-and-pencil tests. The trick here is to avoid tests that discriminate against people with poor reading skills. Attitudes are the hardest to assess. Many instruments are available to measure one's values, styles, and perceptions of organizational climate. But validity and reliability should always be questioned. Skills are either physical (manual dexterity, visual acuity, clerical aptitude) or mental (reasoning, problem solving, planning and organizing). Physical skills can be directly observed—on the job or in a simulation. Mental skills can be measured via paper-and-pencil (case method, tests, simulation).

8. **Entering behavior and terminal behavior.** The KAS that a person has on entering a training program is known as entering behavior. The KAS they require after training so as to do their job effectively is known as terminal behavior. A needs assessment should determine both the entering and the terminal levels of KAS. Assessing the entering KAS is relatively easy. It exists, and is there for the taking. Establishing the terminal KAS is much more difficult, however. It may never have existed before, and a degree of creativity might be necessary to (a) specify certain knowledge, attitudes, or skills that have never been taught before; and (b) sell management on devoting classroom time to it.

For example, management development programs during the 1940s and 1950s focused heavily on reading and writing skills. Then, in the early 1960s, studies on how managers spend their time came out indicating that listening and speaking account for 75% of a manager's communications; reading and writing involve only 25%. And we had never been taught the skills of effective listening, speaking, and interpersonal communications. Since then, a wealth of courses have appeared with heavy emphasis on skills that are far more relevant to the needs of managers—needs that were always there, but no one had shown the creativity or courage to break with tradition and assess them, then teach them.

9. **Reinforcers and constraints.** A needs assessment should examine the workplace environment and take inventory of the reinforcers and constraints—the factors that help or hinder a person returning from training as they attempt to apply what they've just learned. These factors include people, policies, procedures, programs, and physical layout.

Data on these workplace factors can be obtained relatively easily. One method is unobtrusive—what Peters and Waterman refer to as "management by walking around." In their book *In Search of Excellence,* they point out that one of the most important activities in well-managed organizations is walking around, talking informally with employees, making unobtrusive observations of the reinforcers and constraints that are operating in the workplace. Another useful method involves group interviews with a half-dozen employees at a time.

10. **Many methods; not just one.** Our discussion of the preceding nine concepts should have led to the conclusion that a comprehensive assessment of bchavior at work requires an assortment of methods (usually three to six) and not just one or two. The more commonly used methods and techniques are discussed in the chapters that follow.

CHAPTER 10

ELEVEN FACTORS TO EVALUATE

Upon completing this chapter you should be able to

◆ determine which of 11 questions should be answered to evaluate a course

◆ distinguish between formative, summative, and correlative evaluations

◆ list the three things an instructor should evaluate before training

◆ give examples to illustrate the two kinds of data used to measure at Level 3

◆ define learning

◆ state why evaluations of the instructor and the course design are appropriate.

The chart on the next page lists 11 questions that trainers often seek answers to in evaluating the impact of their courses. For a given training program, some of these questions will be relevant while others will not.

Since the next 14 chapters deal with the tools and techniques for answering these questions, let's do a little needs analysis to see which ones address your own evaluation efforts. In the last column labeled "Relevance," enter the word *high, low,* or *none* to indicate the relative importance of each question to the type of courses you teach.

LEVEL	QUESTION TO BE ANSWERED	EVALUATION METHODOLOGY	RELEVANCE
1	**1.** How comfortable were participants? Did they like the course?	End-of-course evaluation sheets, follow-up talks with graduates and their managers.	
1	**2.** How relevant was the course to their needs (job, work, responsibilities)?	Ratings of each course objective (performance criteria) by graduates and managers.	
2	**3.** How well did they learn the knowledge that was taught?	Mastery tests, usually paper and pencil, at key checkpoints and end of course.	
2	**4.** How well did they accept the attitudes (values, style) specified in the objectives?	Climate surveys; measures of opinion, values, style; simulation, observation.	
2	**5.** How well did they develop the desired skills?	Observation in simulations (role play, in-basket, lab, workstation)	
2	**6.** How have their competencies changed (knowledge, attitudes, skills)?	Assessment lab, multimedia evaluation of multiple competencies.	
3	**7.** How has performance actually improved at work (hard data)?	Records on file, assessment of related documents, direct observation.	
3	**8.** How has performance perceptually improved at work (soft data)?	Surveys, interviews, reactions, performance in simulations.	
4	**9.** How has training produced a return-on-investment? (Did it pay?)	Cost-benefit analysis to examine money spent and saved (earned, produced).	
These factors correlate with Levels 1-4	**10.** How effective was the delivery (by instructor or self-study)?	Evaluation by an expert qualified and respected enough to have credibility.	
	11. How effective was the design in supporting the objectives?	Evaluation of content, methods, media, strategies by a credible expert.	

Selecting from the Menu

The remainder of this book contains sample evaluation forms for measuring the impact of a training program at the four levels of the Kirkpatrick model that we examined in chapter 1. Some of these forms provide data at more than one level of evaluation, although the majority of them focus on measuring either reactions, learning (acquisition), behavior (workplace practice), or return-on-investment (ROI). Therefore, you should probably consider the use of several evaluation tools to measure the effectiveness of a given course.

The chart you just completed by ranking the relevance of the 11 questions should serve as your guide as you select from our menu of tools and techniques. These questions fall into natural clusters, as described in the comments that follow. You'll probably want to refer back to the chart as you read this page.

Questions 1 and 2 give the trainees' reactions to the course, and can usually be answered on an end-of-course evaluation sheet. Chapters 11 and 12 address this.

Questions 3, 4, and 5 are concerned with the learning that took place during a training program. Learning can be measured as changes in knowledge, attitudes, and skills (chapters 13, 14, and 15, respectively).

Question 6 deals with competencies, the combination of knowledge, attitudes, and skills in ways that support the duties and responsibilities associated with a given job or group of jobs. Many organizations have moved toward competency-based training and assessment. Chapter 16 addresses competency-based assessment.

Questions 7 and 8 are concerned with performance in the workplace following training. Sometimes the improvement can be documented with hard data (see chapter 17 for numerical measures of training's impact). Sometimes we want to measure improvement with soft data (see chapter 18).

Question 9 addresses the economics of training. Was money spent or invested in the training program? What was the payback period and the ROI? How can one do a cost-benefit analysis? Chapters 19, 20, 21, and 22 address these questions and illustrate several methods of determining ROI.

Question 10 deals with instructor evaluation. This should correlate with ratings on Kirkpatrick's four levels, since good instructors should score better than poor instructors on reactions and on performance during training and in the workplace. Chapter 23 presents forms and techniques for evaluating the instructor.

Question 11 deals with the course design. Like question 10, a professional evaluation should be done by an expert and not by the trainees, who probably lack the criteria to evaluate on any basis other than whether they liked it. Chapter 24 outlines the criteria and presents tools for evaluating the course design.

Chapter 25 deals with preparing and publicizing your evaluation report. Chapter 26 enables you to assess yourself on six instructional competencies.

The pages that follow show how the questions we've just examined contribute either to formative or summative evaluations. A third category, correlative evaluations, serves as the catch-all heading on our menu. It includes any evaluation of the component parts of an instructional system: course design, instructor's delivery, facilities, length of program. At the end of this chapter, you'll find a discussion of 12 lessons on how to evaluate training as well as a representation of the Abstraction Ladder.

The Evaluation of Training

Trainers need to know how well they are doing; how well they are meeting their course objectives; how well their trainees are acquiring the course content; how relevant this content is to their job and their needs outside the classroom; how the trainees are reacting to the course (subject matter, instructional methods, pacing, length); and what organizational performance improvement can be attributed to training.

Senior management also wants to know what return they are getting on the training investment. Firms like General Motors, IBM, and AT&T spend close to a billion dollars annually on training. Dozens of other organizations count their costs of employee training in millions of dollars. The management of HRD is evolving from an "arts and crafts" mode into a technology in which the costs and the benefits of training are scrutinized by the same steely eyes that allocate funds to other investments of the organization's time and resources. They measure worth by looking at the return on each investment.

There are three categories of behavior to be measured when evaluating training. Every trainer must decide which of these is important, and collect data accordingly. Here are the three:

Formative evaluation. Here we are measuring the learner's progress and the degree to which our learning objectives are and aren't being met. The focus here is on mediating (enabling, classroom) behavior and the attainment of new knowledge, attitudes, and skills that can be shaped and observed during training. These measures are of primary value to the trainee and the instructor as input to their efficient management of the learning process. Formative evaluations are conducted before training (to establish bench levels of the learner's entering behavior), during training (to diagnose needs), and at the end of training (to document the acquisition of new knowledge, attitudes, and skills).

Summative evaluation. Here we are measuring the learner's performance after training and the degree to which the behavior back at work meets the expectations that prompted the training. The focus here is on job standards, performance criteria, productivity measures, and the attainment of organizational objectives. These behaviors must be observed and measured in the workplace, where many reinforcers and constraints are influencing the trainee's performance. Thus we are measuring transfer of training and not simply acquisition. These measures are of primary value to line managers and those responsible for the allocation of training resources. Conscientious instructors are also concerned with summative evaluation.

Correlative evaluation. Here we are concerned with evaluating those aspects of course design and delivery that should correlate with the formative and summative measures of performance. The focus here is on course content (relevance, clarity, timeliness); course design (appropriateness of methods, media, time allocation, flow); and delivery (instructor's skills, pacing, responsiveness to needs, how learners felt about the instructor or other delivery systems used). Thus we are measuring means rather than ends—the means used to shape the learner's formative and summative performance. These measures are of primary value to the instructor and course designer as input to revisions or modifications before the course is next offered.

To summarize, formative evaluations measure the learner's progress during training. Summative evaluations measure the learner's performance after training and in the workplace. And correlative evaluation measures the performance of the instructional system (how well the course designer and instructor have fulfilled their respective responsibilities).

Twelve Lessons on How to Evaluate Training

1. **Evaluation must start before you train—afterward is too late.** There are a number of reasons why evaluation must begin with the needs analysis before you design or conduct training: (a) to get commitment on what to evaluate (course objectives) and how to evaluate after training; (b) to measure gain and document your impact (premeasurement and postmeasurement improvements); (c) to identify reinforcers and constraints in the workplace that will help or hinder your graduates in applying what they learned; (d) so you can get agreement on expectations of the managers of your trainees; (e) so you can start to develop a maintenance system that will support and reinforce the desired behavior back on the job.

2. **You must evaluate three things before you train.** First, evaluate the entering behavior of the trainees (EB). What knowledge, attitudes, and skills do they bring that you can build on? Next, evaluate the needs and expectations of the organization, then establish the terminal behavior (TB) that you expect of the trainees after training. Finally, evaluate the workplace in which trainees are expected to perform to see what factors will support or extinguish the desired behavior, so that you can maximize the reinforcers and minimize the constraints. Trainers are gap fillers, closing the gap between EB and TB. Thus, they must know both if they are to evaluate the effectiveness of training.

3. **Evaluation must be an integral part of the instructional process.** Unlike the public schools, where evaluation is done mainly through tests, training sessions should provide maximum oppor-

tunity for hands-on learning and frequent responses by trainees. This gives trainer and trainee alike the frequent feedback they both need to ensure that the learning objectives are being met. By teaching more deductively, using small group exercises, and being learner centered, the trainer does not need a lot of formal testing to evaluate progress. This can be done informally at each class. Such a course design is more efficient (better use of group time), more pleasant (few people like tests, instructors included), and more effective (it produces higher levels of performance).

4. **Formal evaluation should be done by someone besides the trainer.** Instructors have a vested interest in getting high evaluations. Moreover, they can develop end-of-course tests and rating sheets to show anything they want. Thus, the tools and techniques of evaluation should be developed by professionals, and the process of evaluation should be supervised by impartial persons—a training advisory committee of line managers or an outside consultant. Data collected by the trainee and his or her manager is often more acceptable than the trainer's evaluation data.

5. **An up-front performance contract makes evaluation easier.** Effective training is the responsibility of three persons: trainer, trainee, and the trainee's manager. All three must agree on the expected outcomes and on when and how they will be measured. All three must perform if the desired outcomes are to be met. By agreeing at the start on roles and responsibilities, the training will be more effective, the outcomes will be easier to evaluate, the criteria will be agreed upon in advance, and the responsibility for evaluation will have been established.

6. **Delayed evaluation is better.** Although it's easier to evaluate trainees while they are still captive, we can evaluate only their mediating (enabling) behavior in class. If we're interested in transfer of training (from class to job), then we must go to the workplace and take our evaluation measurements after the intervening variables (reinforcers and constraints) have had their impact on the trainee's performance. Some trainers will say: "That's not my department. I have no control over what happens after training." But the strong trend in HRD is toward an organization development (OD) approach that starts with workplace behavior and regards workshop behavior as a subset and supportive (mediating, enabling) element.

7. **The higher we train, the harder it is to evaluate the results.** Employees at lower levels of the organization chart are relatively easy to evaluate. Job standards and expectations are clearer, more quantitative, more observable. But as we move into professional and managerial positions, evaluating the results of training becomes more difficult. Indeed, in many instances the trainee and his or her manager bear the primary responsibility for giving the trainer feedback on the effectiveness of training. The trainer's role is to help them to define *effectiveness* in operational terms rather than in ratings of relevance, timeliness, or popularity.

8. **There are 11 questions to be answered when we evaluate.** Often the trainer lacks the time, need, or trainee tolerance to answer all of them. Thus, we must decide what objectives we wish to accomplish by evaluating before we decide which of the questions we want to answer. Here are some of the reasons for evaluating: to give remedial instruction, to redesign parts of the course, to improve the delivery, to justify the expenditure, to promote the program, to maintain new behaviors back on the job. Of the 11 questions to be answered, three are formative, four are summative, and four are correlative.

9. **There are five levels on the Abstraction Ladder** (see chart at end of chapter). Where do we collect our evaluation data? Where should we take our readings? Our data will range from hard to soft, from fact to opinion, from experience to abstractions of it depending on how far up or down the ladder we choose to evaluate. At the bottom is concrete experience on the job—performance at work. Next comes simulation, where we rate the trainee's own performance. Next comes evaluation of the trainee's response to situations via case method or situational analysis. This is often vicarious rather than personal. Next comes appraisal by others—peers, boss, subordinates, customers. Finally, there are verbal abstractions of reality, where trainees describe the correct and incorrect behavior in response to questions or situations.

10. **We don't know what we don't know.** Perhaps the biggest lesson to be learned on evaluation is the realization that we know what we know, but we don't know what we don't know. Hence, evaluation via any method other than direct observation of hard data back on the job is going to be suspect and shaky. Questionnaires, interviews, and survey research are peripheral to the central issue of evaluation: Can we see improved performance on the job in objective, measurable ways? Hence the current interest in competency-based instruction and in assessment in which trainees respond to real-world stimuli rather than classroom stimuli.

11. **Respondents will often say what they think you want to hear.** Any form of survey research (questionnaires, interviews) faces this reality. Thus, your trainees and their managers find it easy to take the path of least resistance and give good evaluations to your course. It is more difficult to be objective and analytical in assessing a course and its impact. The questions must be specific, unbiased, and open ended enough to accommodate for a full range of ratings.

12. **Evaluation should yield cost and benefit data for senior management.** Although trainers are interested in formative and correlative evaluation data, the bottom-line results that senior management wants to see can be answered only through summative evaluation. This is the most difficult of the three types of measurements, since it must be done in the workplace where the person who has been trained must deal with many constraints that affect transfer of training and the degree of return on the training investment.

THE ABSTRACTION LADDER

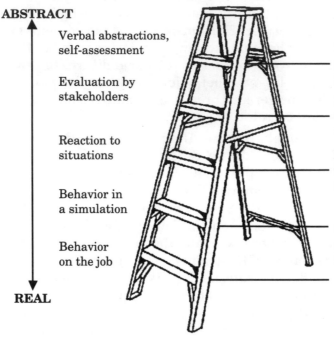

ABSTRACT

Verbal abstractions,
self-assessment

Evaluation by
stakeholders

Reaction to
situations

Behavior in
a simulation

Behavior
on the job

REAL

Trainee evaluates self in
response to questions or
personality trait lists

Manager, peers, work group
evaluate trainees against list
of criteria

Evaluation of trainee's analysis
(case method script for analysis,
situational assessments)

Observation of performance during
simulation (role play, assessment
lab, survival exercise)

Observation of performance at
work (shopper's survey,
performance appraisals,
360-degree survey)

CHAPTER 11

RATING THE COMFORT LEVEL

Upon completing this chapter you should be able to

◆ list at least eight factors affecting the comfort of trainees

◆ give three benefits of determining the participants' comfort level

◆ state the benefits of rating sheets at end of course and one month thereafter

◆ select from three examples the rating sheet(s) best suited to your course(s).

When we ask participants to complete an end-of-course evaluation sheet, we're attempting to measure at Level 1: "Did they like it?" Their ratings are strongly influenced by their comfort level. (We know of one training manager who asked every hotel or conference facility where he ran his five-day workshops to be sure to "give 'em steak and wine on Thursday." This was a sure-fire way of improving the end-of-course ratings!)

The comfort of your participants is influenced by many factors. Some of the major ones are as follows:

◆ Pacing. Did the course move too fast, too slow, or about right?

◆ Selection of participants. Was the group cohesive, or were there misfits?

◆ Facilities. How comfortable were the room, chairs, decor, location, traffic?

◆ Breaks. Length, frequency, availability of refreshments?

◆ Instructor(s). Pleasing personality, good humor, relaxed, easy to understand?

◆ Meals. Provided? Good local restaurants? Enough time to eat and meet?

◆ Course materials. Quality appearance, user-friendly, convey sense of worth?

◆ Surprise free. Agenda, objectives, breaks, timing known in advance?

◆ Participation. Sufficient interaction and hands-on practice?

◆ Motivation to attend. Voluntary or required? Treat or treatment?

◆ Work outside class. Was prework or homework manageable or excessive?

◆ Conflicting priorities. Was participant free of crisis at home or at work?

Many other factors influence the comfort level of your participants, but the dozen listed above are frequently cited by participants when asked to explain their ratings. Why do we care about such factors? Why don't we simply focus on delivering a quality training program? After all, we're not in the entertainment business or the facilities management business. Why worry about the comfort level of the participants? We care because (a) participants will learn better if they are more comfortable; (b) discomfort is a distraction; (c) you want your graduates to be promoters and boosters of the course to others who haven't taken it yet; (d) participants who like the course are more likely to apply it at work; (e) it's no fun trying to teach a group of uncomfortable, dissatisfied participants.

The Universally Popular Smile Sheet

By far the most widely used end-of-course evaluation tool is the smile sheet, given to participants just before a training program is adjourned. The ratings asked for can be quantified easily, making the trainer's job easier in analyzing and tallying the data.

When courses are short (one day or less), these evaluation forms should be distributed and collected at the very end of the program. On courses that are longer (three days or more), a strong case can be made for asking for the evaluations before people are anxious to "hit the road"—perhaps during the lunch break of the last day rather than during the last 10 minutes of the course. It's generally not a good idea to let participants take the sheets with them and send them back, since this puts you in the business of telephoning and hounding them to return the forms. If you want to evaluate a program's relevance to the workplace and the degree of transfer that took place following training, then it's appropriate to mail an evaluation form to participants a month or so after the training program.

The pages that follow contain three examples of smile sheets. The first two are designed for use during the final half-hour of a course. The third, titled Manager's Assessment of Progress, is sent to two parties: the participant and the participant's immediate supervisor. (In this example, both are managers who are being asked to evaluate the impact of a management development program.)

Evaluation Form

For use by participants—to be turned in at the completion of the session.

Please indicate your reaction to the session by placing an X in the column that best expresses your rating of each of the following:

	Excellent	Good	Average	Adequate	Poor
Coverage of the informative material (concepts, facts, principles, procedures, knowledge)					
Applicability to your own job, responsibilities, and needs					
Sufficient examples and chances to practice so that you are able to apply these new skills back at work					
Appropriate use of instructional methods and media so that learning was easy and enjoyable					
Opportunity for discussion with other participants to exchange experience and ideas					
Instructor's manner and ability to hold your interest and to impart new concepts and skills					
Length of the program relative to its objectives and the needs of the group					
Sufficient information in advance of the session so that you knew what to expect					
Appropriate selection of participants so that you were sharing the experience with others of similar need					
Taking into account all aspects of the session, please give us your overall rating.					

In your opinion, what was the strongest aspect of the session?

What suggestions do you have for improving the sessions?

Name (Optional): _____   Location: _____

Honestly, Now ...

We'd like you to evaluate the course. A list of modules that were offered appears below. In the box preceding each module that you attended, place the number 1, 2, or 3 to indicate your rating. Before doing this, place an X in the box of each module that was not presented or that you did not attend. Here is what the numbers represent:

1 = Very useful; I found this to be quite helpful.
2 = Somewhat useful, but could be stronger.
3 = Not useful; I found little of help to me.
X = Module not given or not attended.

Part One: Course Content

❑ Motivation: Why People Work

❑ Communication: Process in Perspective

❑ The Dynamics of Face-to-Face Communication

❑ Performance Appraisal: Guidelines for Evaluating Human Performance

❑ Training and Coaching: Steps to Improved Performance

❑ Applied Transactional Analysis

❑ Managing Your Time Effectively

❑ Running Effective Meetings and Conferences

❑ Listening: Sharpening Your Analytical Skills

❑ Styles of Management

❑ Writing More Effective Letters, Memos, and Reports

❑ Career Planning

❑ Conducting Effective Selection Interviews

❑ Setting Goals and Standards

❑ Skills for Negotiation and Conflict Management

❑ Planning, Scheduling, and Controlling the Work

❑ Your Role in Administering Personnel Policies and Procedures

❑ Making Presentations and Selling Ideas

❑ Productivity and Performance Improvement

❑ Team Building

❑ Problem Solving

❑ Decision Making

Part Two: Instructional Methods

Our design of the course included a number of instructional methods and media. These are listed below. In front of each, place the number 1, 2, or 3 to indicate your rating. Behind each we've provided space for you to make any recommendations for improvements.

❑ cassette and workbook (self-study) _____

❑ case study _____

❑ role play _____

❑ critical incident _____

❑ script analysis _____

❑ meetings with boss _____

❑ self-assessment _____

❑ games/simulations _____

❑ videotapes _____

❑ action plans _____

Part Three: Additional Comments

Use the space below to enter any comments or suggestions you have relating to the length of class, time and place of meetings, size of group, selection of participants, or any other aspects of how the course was handled.

Your overall evaluation of the course (check one):

❑ Excellent   ❑ Very Good   ❑ Good   ❑ Fair   ❑ Poor

Your name (optional): 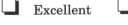_____

Manager's Assessment of Progress

☐ Participant: _____

☐ Participant's Manager: _____

Place a check mark in the box to indicate who completed this form.

During the management development program just completed, the two of you had certain expectations and outcomes in mind at the start of the program. Now it is time to take inventory and measure the degree to which your expectations have or have not been met. Please answer the five questions below without conferring with one another. Then, after completing this sheet, you may wish to compare answers and discuss your evaluation of the program.

1. Think back to your preprogram expectations, reservations, desires. On a scale of 1 to 10, with 1 being "extremely negative" and 10 being "extremely positive," what number best expresses your feelings back at the start of the course: _____

   Please explain why: _____

   _____

   _____

   _____

   _____

   _____

2. Now that the program is several months behind us, what number best expresses your current feelings on its value: _____

   Please explain why: _____

   _____

   _____

   _____

   _____

   _____

3. What do you see as the major benefits gained from the program (be specific please):

   _____

   _____

   _____

   _____

   _____

   _____

4. What changes would you recommend in the design of the program to make future cycles more effective (be specific please): _____

_____

_____

_____

_____

_____

_____

_____

_____

5. Taking into account all the expenses associated with the program (course materials, instructor, salary of participants, meeting facilities), the investment probably amounts to something in the range of $1,000 per participant. If we view this as an investment, what figure would you guess might represent the return on this investment over the next three years: $_____. Please explain why. (We recognize that there is no precise way to measure return-on-investment on management development, and that questions like this can cause sleepless nights for engineers and accountants! However, who is in a better position than you to answer? So, please give us the benefit of your thinking.):

_____

_____

_____

_____

_____

_____

_____

_____

Thanks for taking the time to respond. Your feedback helps us to strengthen the program and make it better for future participants.

CHAPTER 12

RATING COURSE RELEVANCY

Upon completing this chapter you should be able to

◆ show how the evaluation of relevancy differs for new and veteran employees

◆ state at least four ways to improve training's relevancy

◆ list the pros and cons of two sample evaluation forms

◆ select from two samples the one that is better suited to your course.

Although the trend these days seems to be toward selecting instructors who have performed the tasks or jobs they will be teaching, there are still many trainers who design, develop, or deliver courses to teach concepts or skills with which they've had little personal experience. This puts them at a disadvantage in bridging the gap between the course content and its relevancy to the trainee's workplace or past experience.

As trainers, we may be sold on the relevance of the concepts, tools, techniques, and procedures that we teach. However, relevancy (like beauty) is in the eye of the beholder. If our trainees do not see the course content as relevant to their needs, then our Level 1 ratings ("Did they like it?") will suffer. Here are the types of comments on evaluation sheets that indicate a problem of relevancy:

"The course was interesting but too theoretical and academic."

"At work we don't do things the way we were taught—no time."

"The instructors really don't understand what it's like out there."

"You don't need to know all this stuff to be good at your job."

If you're training newly hired employees, they have no basis for evaluating the relevancy of the course. In such cases it's better to give them a month or so on the job before asking them to complete an evaluation form that assesses relevancy. When relevancy is low, the instructor's credibility will suffer and participants will feel that the course was a waste of time. What can be done to improve relevancy? Here are a few ideas:

◆ Deliver just-in-time training with no delay between learning and applying.

◆ Select instructors who are experienced and who can relate to trainees.

◆ Use action plans; after each topic, have trainees indicate how they'll apply it.

◆ Put new hires on the job to observe for a day or so before starting training.

◆ Convert each concept, policy, or theory into a practical application.

◆ Make course design more participative, interactive; more hands-on learning.

◆ Have participants add each task they learn to their job description.

The Responsibility for Relevancy

Trainees who are new to the job or the organization are not prepared to give the instructor feedback on the relevancy (applicability, usefulness, value) of the information they receive during training. Only in the months that follow training will they know how relevant the course was to their needs at work. In contrast, trainees who have held the job and are learning supplementary concepts and procedures can often be quite effective in evaluating their relevancy. In such courses, the instructor should establish this mutual dependency at the start of the program by saying something like:

> "During this workshop you'll be learning a lot of new things that should make you more effective at work, provided the information and techniques I have to offer you are relevant to your work. And this is where I need your help, since you bring a wealth of experience into the classroom. I'd like you to assume responsibility for making sure that every fact, skill, concept, procedure, and technique that I give you is relevant to your job. The moment you question the usefulness of my information, raise your hand and challenge it. My responsibility is to demonstrate its value or, that failing, to remove it from the course. Can I count on you?"

The ultimate responsibility for course relevancy rests with the instructor who should be evaluating its relevancy throughout the training program. How? By having participants complete action plans. By asking questions ("Now, how does this apply back on the job? When would you put this into action at work?"). By creating hands-on learning situations to see if they can apply new learning. Relevancy also can be measured after training is completed. The pages that follow contain two such examples:

The Professional Trainer. This form is sent to participants prior to a workshop. They complete column A and return the form (needs analysis). Then, after the workshop, it is given back to the participants with the request that they complete column B. This technique enables the instructor to see which topics are seen as more relevant and less relevant than before, and to record the difference as an increase (+) or decrease (−) in column C.

PAR: Proficiency Assessment Report. This type of form can be used before training to assess need and following training to measure change in the perception of participants and their managers. This example relates to supervisory or managerial skills, but the format could be used in many types of courses by creating a description of the skills and abilities associated with each major topic (subset) of a course, then asking participants and their supervisors to assign ratings to relevance and proficiency.

The Professional Trainer

Listed below are 20 of our learning objectives. Your job is to indicate in column A the relative importance or interest of each to you, using a five-point scale with 5 standing for "very important" and 1 meaning "no importance or interest." Do not attempt to have a normal distribution. Your ratings could be all fives, ones, or any combination. Ignore columns B and C.

After this workshop you will be able to

	A	B	C

1. employ the appropriate tools and techniques of needs analysis to determine the needs of learners, before and during a course

2. state the objectives of any training session in a way that satisfies six criteria of a complete behavioral objective

3. establish the entering behavior of learners: their experience, knowledge, attitudes, skills, and expectations relating to the course

4. break down information (stimulus, or S), with responses (R) and feedback (F) after each S, thereby forming a chain of SRF links

5. prepare a behavioral analysis of any task or procedure, identifying the needed knowledge-attitudes-skills

6. select methods and media appropriate to each of the five stages of an instructional system, from preparation to maintenance

7. describe the benefits and limitations of at least five input and five output instructional methods

8. write course materials (handouts, notebooks, learning exercises) in a clear, crisp, interesting manner

9. create visual aids (transparencies, flipcharts, slides) with effective graphics, color, organization, and flow

10. describe and apply at least 10 techniques for getting a high level of participation from all learners and not just the verbal few

11. phrase questions effectively so as to get all learners responding and to elicit relevant responses that show application and not just acquisition of knowledge

12. use discussion leadership skills effectively (summary statements, probes, and other directive and nondirective techniques)

13. deal effectively with different types of problem participants to maintain a positive climate and meet the learning objectives

14. analyze your instructional style and its appropriateness to type of student, subject matter, teaching method, and personality

15. teach inductively (lecture) and deductively (Socratic), indicating when and how to use each method

16. identify at least eight workplace factors that jeopardize transfer of training and describe how to deal with each

17. carry out a cost-benefit analysis that can be used to evaluate feasibility (before design) and impact (after training)

18. strengthen transfer of training from class to workplace, using at least five of the 20 techniques taught

19. evaluate instruction against 10 questions (criteria) that establish the course's effectiveness at four levels

20. prepare the person(s) responsible for delivering training and maintaining performance (instructors, supervisors, team members).

PAR: Proficiency Assessment Report

This exercise is designed to help supervisors and managers determine their proficiency on a series of abilities commonly associated with effective management. It enables supervisors to rate themselves and to have the immediate boss rate the supervisors also. This information is then used as a basis for training and development, and as a benchmark against which future growth and improvement can be compared.

Here's how the exercise works. For each paragraph describing a skills cluster, you should assign two ratings. The first indicates the **relevance,** or how important this group of skills is to the job now held by the supervisor. The second rating indicates the **proficiency,** or competence of the supervisor on the skills cluster. The same scale, from 5 to 1, is used on both ratings:

5 = Extremely   4 = Above Average   3 = Average   2 = Below Average   1 = Negligible

These five numbers appear in two sets of boxes. Place an X in the box that best reflects your perception of the person you are rating, both on relevance and on proficiency. Thus, if you felt that the skills cluster was extremely relevant and that the proficiency was average, your ratings would look like this:

RELEVANCE

PROFICIENCY

---

1. Managing Time Effectively

Ability to manage time, both your own and the time of others with whom you work. Includes such skills as making a daily "to do" list; prioritizing based on the relative weight assigned to importance and urgency; keeping a weekly time log; investing time rather than spending it; delegating or getting help on the basis of the cost of your time vs. theirs.

RELEVANCE

5	4	3	2	1

PROFICIENCY

5	4	3	2	1

2. Communication in Perspective

Ability to analyze the factors that spell success in all methods of communication: speaking, listening, reading, and writing. Includes the following concepts and skills: matching the purpose(s) of each person involved in the communication; separating message from method of delivery; 10 reasons for communicating; overcoming the barriers to effective communication; applying a three-step communication model.

RELEVANCE

5	4	3	2	1

PROFICIENCY

5	4	3	2	1

3. Conducting Performance Reviews

Ability to plan and carry out a constructive performance appraisal. Includes the following skills: having both parties prepare for the interview; eliminating the major problems in conducting appraisals (up to 20); applying a seven-step process for analyzing performance deficiencies; using a job description as a basis for performance reviews; giving correction in a constructive manner; applying specific steps (up to 12) in planning and conducting a satisfying, results-oriented review.

RELEVANCE

5	4	3	2	1

PROFICIENCY

5	4	3	2	1

4. Interacting Face to Face

Ability to influence the thinking and behavior of others through interpersonal communication. Includes the following skills: controlling aim (purpose), bias (influence), and climate (rapport); using probes to get more information; distinguishing between direct and hidden meanings; overcoming barriers to communication; using directive and nondirective questions appropriately; planning an interaction in advance.

RELEVANCE

5	4	3	2	1

PROFICIENCY

5	4	3	2	1

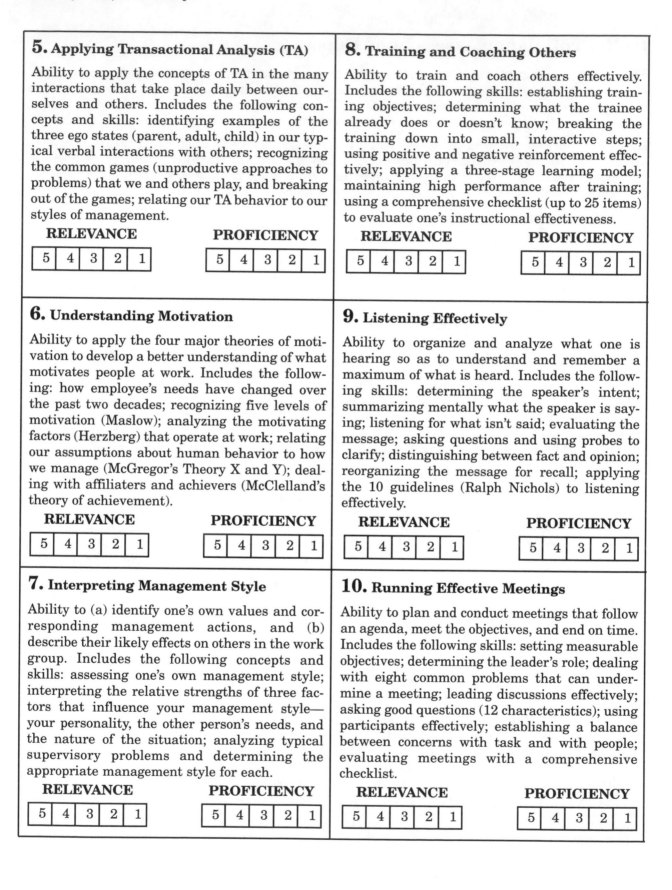

5. **Applying Transactional Analysis (TA)**

Ability to apply the concepts of TA in the many interactions that take place daily between ourselves and others. Includes the following concepts and skills: identifying examples of the three ego states (parent, adult, child) in our typical verbal interactions with others; recognizing the common games (unproductive approaches to problems) that we and others play, and breaking out of the games; relating our TA behavior to our styles of management.

RELEVANCE

| 5 | 4 | 3 | 2 | 1 |

PROFICIENCY

| 5 | 4 | 3 | 2 | 1 |

6. **Understanding Motivation**

Ability to apply the four major theories of motivation to develop a better understanding of what motivates people at work. Includes the following: how employee's needs have changed over the past two decades; recognizing five levels of motivation (Maslow); analyzing the motivating factors (Herzberg) that operate at work; relating our assumptions about human behavior to how we manage (McGregor's Theory X and Y); dealing with affiliaters and achievers (McClelland's theory of achievement).

RELEVANCE

| 5 | 4 | 3 | 2 | 1 |

PROFICIENCY

| 5 | 4 | 3 | 2 | 1 |

7. **Interpreting Management Style**

Ability to (a) identify one's own values and corresponding management actions, and (b) describe their likely effects on others in the work group. Includes the following concepts and skills: assessing one's own management style; interpreting the relative strengths of three factors that influence your management style—your personality, the other person's needs, and the nature of the situation; analyzing typical supervisory problems and determining the appropriate management style for each.

RELEVANCE

| 5 | 4 | 3 | 2 | 1 |

PROFICIENCY

| 5 | 4 | 3 | 2 | 1 |

8. **Training and Coaching Others**

Ability to train and coach others effectively. Includes the following skills: establishing training objectives; determining what the trainee already does or doesn't know; breaking the training down into small, interactive steps; using positive and negative reinforcement effectively; applying a three-stage learning model; maintaining high performance after training; using a comprehensive checklist (up to 25 items) to evaluate one's instructional effectiveness.

RELEVANCE

| 5 | 4 | 3 | 2 | 1 |

PROFICIENCY

| 5 | 4 | 3 | 2 | 1 |

9. **Listening Effectively**

Ability to organize and analyze what one is hearing so as to understand and remember a maximum of what is heard. Includes the following skills: determining the speaker's intent; summarizing mentally what the speaker is saying; listening for what isn't said; evaluating the message; asking questions and using probes to clarify; distinguishing between fact and opinion; reorganizing the message for recall; applying the 10 guidelines (Ralph Nichols) to listening effectively.

RELEVANCE

| 5 | 4 | 3 | 2 | 1 |

PROFICIENCY

| 5 | 4 | 3 | 2 | 1 |

10. **Running Effective Meetings**

Ability to plan and conduct meetings that follow an agenda, meet the objectives, and end on time. Includes the following skills: setting measurable objectives; determining the leader's role; dealing with eight common problems that can undermine a meeting; leading discussions effectively; asking good questions (12 characteristics); using participants effectively; establishing a balance between concerns with task and with people; evaluating meetings with a comprehensive checklist.

RELEVANCE

| 5 | 4 | 3 | 2 | 1 |

PROFICIENCY

| 5 | 4 | 3 | 2 | 1 |

11. Writing to Get Results

Ability to write letters, memos, and reports that are crisp and compelling, getting the desired action from the reader(s). Includes the following skills: determining the purpose of the message in measurable terms; selecting content, format, and style; applying the six Cs of effective writing: clarity, completeness, conciseness, character, courtesy, and control; translating business jargon into simpler conversational equivalents; measuring the effectiveness of past and future writing.

RELEVANCE

| 5 | 4 | 3 | 2 | 1 |

PROFICIENCY

| 5 | 4 | 3 | 2 | 1 |

12. Career Planning

Ability to take inventory, to explore career options and directions, and to develop an action plan for achieving life goals. Includes the following concepts and skills: preparing a life planning chart; assessing work-related feelings (up to 20 items) and assumptions (up to 12 items) about career planning; analyzing strengths and weaknesses in boss-subordinate relationships; assessing one's personal values; exploring 12 options for increased career mobility at work.

RELEVANCE

| 5 | 4 | 3 | 2 | 1 |

PROFICIENCY

| 5 | 4 | 3 | 2 | 1 |

13. Conducting Selection Interviews

Ability to prepare for and conduct a selection interview that draws out the information needed to reach a sound hiring decision. Includes the following skills: analyzing the position; determining the skills, values, and traits needed to perform the job; analyzing the application form data; generating appropriate questions; avoiding illegal questions (EEO and eliminating personal bias); planning a structured but conversational interview; meeting specific criteria that lead to a final selection decision.

RELEVANCE

| 5 | 4 | 3 | 2 | 1 |

PROFICIENCY

| 5 | 4 | 3 | 2 | 1 |

14. Setting Goals and Standards

Ability to manage activities and projects toward measurable goals and standards, setting these jointly with others so as to develop their understanding and commitment. Includes the following skills: distinguishing among wishes, activities, goals, standards, and quotas; reducing barriers to the goal-setting process; identifying characteristics of task-oriented and goal-oriented persons and how to deal with each; evaluating goals against a half-dozen criteria; using goals to motivate.

RELEVANCE

| 5 | 4 | 3 | 2 | 1 |

PROFICIENCY

| 5 | 4 | 3 | 2 | 1 |

15. Planning, Scheduling, Controlling

Ability to manage projects, (one-time programs) and processes (ongoing work flow) by applying the major tools and techniques of management. Includes the following skills: using Program Evaluation and Review Techniques (PERT) to plan, schedule, and control a series of activities so as to meet the predetermined goals on time and within budget; preparing flowcharts to analyze and communicate processes; applying techniques to simplify major tasks; dealing with resistance to change.

RELEVANCE

| 5 | 4 | 3 | 2 | 1 |

PROFICIENCY

| 5 | 4 | 3 | 2 | 1 |

16. Negotiation

Ability to negotiate so that both parties accept the outcome. (The negotiation skills referred to here are not primarily for union-management negotiations, but for resolving interpersonal differences.) Includes the following skills: determining the needs and desired outcomes of each party; preparing for negotiation (seven steps); selecting appropriate strategies (12 alternatives); applying five ways to manage conflict; determining when to manage and when to resolve conflict.

RELEVANCE

| 5 | 4 | 3 | 2 | 1 |

PROFICIENCY

| 5 | 4 | 3 | 2 | 1 |

17. **Administering Personnel Policies**

Ability to interpret the organization's policies and procedures to subordinates, and to administer them fairly and legally. Includes the following knowledge and skills: understanding the needs of today's employees; avoiding a rule-book approach; using discipline effectively; dealing correctly with drugs, alcohol, pregnancy, absenteeism, tardiness, vacation, leaves of absence, sick days, tuition refund, accidents or sickness at work, overtime, reimbursements, salary reviews, soliciting at work.

RELEVANCE

5	4	3	2	1

PROFICIENCY

5	4	3	2	1

18. **Making Effective Presentations**

Ability to prepare and deliver well-organized presentations. Includes the following skills: establishing the need and interest level of the audience (whether one person or a group); planning a tailored presentation; building interest and confidence at the start; converting features into benefits; using examples and analogies to improve retention; dealing with questions and objections; preparing physically and psychologically; evaluating a presentation against specific criteria (up to 20).

RELEVANCE

5	4	3	2	1

PROFICIENCY

5	4	3	2	1

19. **Improving Productivity**

Ability to involve members of the work group in a program to improve productivity by increasing output, decreasing input, or both. Includes the following skills: measuring the productivity potential of an operation or work group; determining how to track productivity; overcoming resistance to change; selecting the appropriate action(s) for specific productivity improvement efforts.

RELEVANCE

5	4	3	2	1

PROFICIENCY

5	4	3	2	1

20. **Building Teamwork**

Ability to develop winning team attitudes, high group member satisfaction, and superior performance levels by applying the concepts and skills of team building. Includes the following: distinguishing between the behavior of coaches and bosses; applying the techniques used by effective coaches; assessing strengths and weaknesses in the work group's ability to function as a team; identifying areas for improvement; implementing a plan of action to strengthen the teamwork.

RELEVANCE

5	4	3	2	1

PROFICIENCY

5	4	3	2	1

21. **Solving Problems**

Ability to (a) identify barriers that keep us from achieving our goals, and (b) apply systematic problem-solving procedures to reduce the root causes. Includes the following: identifying barriers, or problems; defining goals that are not being met; distinguishing between problems and symptoms; identifying probable causes; collecting and weighing evidence; locating the root problem(s); evaluating alternate courses of action; implementing change; evaluating results.

RELEVANCE

5	4	3	2	1

PROFICIENCY

5	4	3	2	1

22. **Making Decisions**

Ability to make decisions in an objective, scientific manner. Includes the following skills: stating the objectives to be obtained by the best decision; specifying the criteria to be applied to options (both the "musts" and the "wants"); generating alternatives; setting values on each criterion and on each alternative; multiplying these values to select the best alternatives (preparing a decision matrix); assessing risk; implementing decisions; monitoring results; using group decision making.

RELEVANCE

5	4	3	2	1

PROFICIENCY

5	4	3	2	1

Summary

Now it's time to summarize. The need for training and development is greatest on those skills clusters that are ranked high on relevance and low on proficiency, as shown.

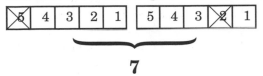

Any skills cluster that has six or more unmarked boxes between your ratings (the example shows seven) indicates a strong need for training and development. On the list below, enter the number of unmarked boxes in front of each title.

____ 1. Managing Time Effectively

____ 2. Communication in Perspective

____ 3. Conducting Performance Reviews

____ 4. Interacting Face to Face

____ 5. Transactional Analysis

____ 6. Understanding Motivation

____ 7. Interpreting Management Style

____ 8. Training and Coaching Others

____ 9. Listening Effectively

____ 10. Running Effective Meetings

____ 11. Writing to Get Results

____ 12. Career Planning

____ 13. Conducting Selection Interviews

____ 14. Setting Goals and Standards

____ 15. Planning, Scheduling, Controlling

____ 16. Negotiation

____ 17. Administering Personnel Policies

____ 18. Making Effective Presentations

____ 19. Improving Productivity

____ 20. Building Teamwork

____ 21. Solving Problems

____ 22. Making Decisions

CHAPTER 13

MEASURING KNOWLEDGE ACQUISITION

Upon completing this chapter you should be able to

◆ list four levels for measuring knowledge, from reception to application

◆ give several examples of training that is almost entirely knowledge based

◆ identify the types of questions used to evaluate knowledge (at least four).

At Level 2 of evaluation, we ask, "How well did they learn it?" Learning is concerned with behavior change in three areas: knowledge, attitudes, and skills. Let's examine knowledge in this section. The other components will follow.

Knowledge is a big umbrella. It takes in facts, concepts, principles, rules, procedures, policy, theory—in short the information component of your course. We measure knowledge at four levels. Each is progressively harder to assess. Here are the levels, along with test items from a course on basic electricity to illustrate each:

◆ Did they receive it?   State Ohm's law.

◆ Do they understand?   Describe the relationship of voltage, current, and resistance.

◆ Have they accepted it?   Indicate how you might use Ohm's law in your work.

◆ Can they apply it?   Draw a circuit diagram to show how you might determine the resistance (ohms) of a light bulb. Include a voltmeter and ammeter in your diagram.

Some courses are heavily dependent on the learner's acquisition of knowledge. Examples include sales training (hundreds of products, thousands of features and benefits) and technical training (computer language, commands). Here we evaluate knowledge. Other courses are light on knowledge and heavier on the other components. Some examples are values clarification, business ethics, the management of personal growth, team building through increased trust, understanding, and cooperation. These words all suggest experiential learning and a strong focus on the attitudinal component of human behavior. Similarly, we can cite examples of courses that focus mainly on the skills component: manufacturing and assembly procedures, the development of manual dexterity (typing), the operation of equipment (milling machine, forklift truck).

In courses where the focus is mainly on changing the learner's attitudes or skills, you may not find it appropriate to measure knowledge gained unless the knowledge is essential to the performance of the attitude or skill back on the job. For example, in safety training, the desired behavior is strongly attitudinal (safe work habits, taking time and not cutting corners), but a heavy knowledge base is essential to producing the desired attitudes (how things work, how accidents are caused, how to lift safely).

Taking another example, this time in the skills area, consider the training of typists. Knowledge of the "home keys" is an important input: fingers of the left hand on *A, S, D, F.* However, this knowledge quickly becomes automatic as typists build up speed, and the experienced typist would look at you strangely if you tried to test knowledge with: "Which finger is used to hit the *J* key?" Or "which are the home keys?"

Calling a Test a Test

Some trainers avoid giving tests. "It's a dirty word to participants," they explain in defense. In courses that rely heavily on knowledge acquisition, however, there's no substitute for a test. Paper-and-pencil tests to measure one's knowledge are the easiest types of evaluation to create and to score. A variety of formats are available: matching questions, sentence completion, multiple choice, essay. These are familiar from our school days. Other formats may be less familiar: in-basket, for example, or having trainees label a diagram or attach labels to a piece of equipment to indicate the names and functions of parts.

The pages that follow contain an example of a test used to measure knowledge in the training field: Assessment of HRD Knowledge. Matching items and sentence completion questions are used extensively in this test.

Assessment of HRD Knowledge

The test is designed to measure your knowledge of the key concepts, contributions, and contributors to the HRD field. It consists of two parts. Each is worth 25 points, for a total possible score of 50 points.

Part One: Contributions to HRD

Listed below are the names of 28 contributors. Most entries contain individual names, although some entries list two names where people have worked as a pair or where several parties have made the same type of contribution to HRD. Their contributions are described in the column to the right, in scrambled sequence. Your job is to select any 25 of the contributors and to identify their contribution by entering the appropriate number in the space preceding their names. If you can't find 25 familiar entries, it is better to go with only those you know than to guess.

Your Selection	Contributors	Contribution
_____	Don Kirkpatrick	1. competency studies
_____	Warren Bennis, A. Zaleznik	2. value programming
_____	Malcolm Knowles	3. front-end analysis
_____	Hall, Pfeiffer, Parry	4. programmed instruction
_____	Joe Harless	5. MBO (management by objectives)
_____	Maslow, Herzberg, McClelland	6. reinforcement theory, behaviorism
_____	Cabot Jaffee, Doug Bray	7. Theory X and Y
_____	Ned Herrmann	8. left brain, right brain, whole brain
_____	Robert Blake, Jane Mouton	9. leadership studies
_____	Douglas McGregor	10. nondirective interviewing
_____	J.L. Bradford, Warner Burke	11. four levels of evaluation
_____	Hubert Wilke, Coleman Finkel	12. adult learning (Andragogy)
_____	Patricia McLagan	13. organizational psychology
_____	Geary Rummler, Tom Gilbert	14. transactional analysis
_____	Jack Zenger	15. consulting and empowerment
_____	Ben Tregoe, Charles Kepner	16. publishers of experiential training
_____	Harry Levinson, Mason Haire	17. the managerial grid
_____	Carl Jung, Myers-Briggs	18. motivation theory
_____	Tony Alessandra, Larry Wilson	19. situational leadership
_____	Robert Mager	20. human performance systems
_____	Peter Drucker, George Odiorne	21. preparing instructional objectives
_____	Peter Block	22. assessment centers
_____	Carl Rogers	23. training facilities design
_____	Morris Massey	24. problem solving, strategic planning
_____	Ken Blanchard, Paul Hersey	25. T-groups, sensitivity training
_____	Eric Berne, Tom Harris	26. psychological types, four patterns
_____	Karen & Dale Brethower	27. behavior modeling
_____	B.F. Skinner, Goodwin Watson	28. sales training

Part Two: Key Concepts in HRD

Answer these eight questions in the space provided immediately after each question. Please print, type, or write clearly. Questions 1 through 7 are worth three points each. The last question is worth four points. Thus, Part Two is worth a total of 25 points.

1. Sensitivity training, or T-groups (NTL, begun in Bethel, Maine) is best described as a form of training in which _____

   _____

   _____

   _____

   _____

   _____

   _____

   _____

2. When placed in class, adults differ from children or adolescents in a number of significant ways that should influence both the design and delivery of instruction. Three of these are (state the implication of each):

   ◆ _____

   _____

   _____

   ◆ _____

   _____

   _____

   ◆ _____

   _____

   _____

3. A number of criteria should be applied whenever a trainer prepares or reviews course objectives. Three of these are:

   ◆ _____

   _____

   _____

   ◆ _____

   _____

   _____

   ◆ _____

   _____

   _____

4. Human behavior during learning can be broken into three components: knowledge, skill, and attitude. Select an example of a course you are familiar with, and show how each of these three elements might best be taught during the course.

Title and brief description of course: _____

_____

_____

_____

Example of a **knowledge** objective and how it might best be taught: _____

_____

_____

_____

_____

Example of a **skill** objective and how it might best be taught: _____

_____

_____

_____

_____

Example of an **attitude** objective and how it might best be taught: _____

_____

_____

_____

_____

5. Suppose you've just been asked to put together a course to teach supervisors how to do performance appraisals effectively. What activities and/or techniques will you use to do the needs analysis prior to designing or purchasing your course materials?

_____

_____

_____

_____

_____

_____

_____

6. Programmed instruction, or self-study courses, have at least three advantages over instructor-based (classroom) training. What are they?

◆ _____

_____

_____

7. There are a number of things the course designer can do to improve transfer of training from workshop to workplace. Name at least three:

◆ _____

_____

_____

8. Many factors are present in the work environment that will help or hinder trainees as they attempt to apply on the job what they learned during class. Some of these are "facts of life" in any organization, and there is little the trainer or trainees can do to overcome them. (Example: having enough time on the job to do things the way they were taught and practiced in class, where there were no conflicting priorities.) But other factors are ones that an effective trainer should know before launching a course, so that they can be addressed in class so as to prepare trainees to deal with them. List at least four such factors that should be looked into during the needs analysis that precedes the launching of a course.

◆ _____

_____

_____

◆ _____

_____

_____

◆ _____

_____

_____

◆ _____

_____

_____

◆ _____

_____

_____

◆ _____

_____

_____

◆ _____

_____

_____

CHAPTER 14

MEASURING ATTITUDE FORMATION

Upon completing this chapter you should be able to

◆ distinguish between overt and covert behavior

◆ describe at least five techniques for evaluating attitudes

◆ describe how each of four leadership styles relates to attitudes

◆ give examples of training that are largely attitudinal in nature.

Of the three components of behavior (knowledge, attitudes, and skills), the most difficult to measure is attitudes. Let's make sure we understand what is meant by attitudes. The term refers to such things as feelings, beliefs, opinions, style, values, and perceptions. Courses that deal with how people relate to themselves and to others are usually concerned with the shaping of attitudes. Examples include assertiveness training, interpersonal relations, personal growth, customer relations, awareness and sensitivity, and employee involvement.

Knowledge and skills are overt, or can easily be brought to the surface. Thus, they can be evaluated by observing the trainee perform: on a paper-and-pencil exercise, a simulation of workplace conditions, or some other arrangement of situations (stimuli) that we present to our trainees and then measure the appropriateness of their reactions (responses). In contrast, attitudes are covert. They can't be seen and it takes more effort to bring them to the surface and more ability on our part to interpret the trainees' responses. Moreover, some attitudes are closely tied to personality, religious beliefs, ideologies, and other "hands-off" areas that trainers and trainees are wary of entering. Fortunately, a lot of progress has been made in measuring attitudes. Here are some techniques used:

◆ **Organizational climate survey:** Measures employee's attitudes toward organizational issues such as clarity of goals, quality of work life, opportunity for growth and advancement; appropriate where courses focus on teamwork, supervisory skills, management development.

- **Employee attitude survey:** Measures employee's attitudes on specific issues and new programs that training is helping to launch. Examples include employee involvement, quality improvement, stress management, and career development.

- **Projective test:** Photos, drawings, or graphic descriptions depict a vague situation to which trainees respond by describing what is happening, how the people feel, and what outcome is likely; measures the attitudes (feelings, reactions) projected into the situation.

- **Critical incident:** Similar to projective test, only the trainee provides the situation from personal experience, then describes feelings and outcomes in reaction to a recent incident.

- **Sentence completion:** Measures reaction to situations by getting trainee to say the first thing that comes to mind. An example of a test item measuring attitudes toward performance appraisal is: "When my boss tells me it's time for my annual performance review, I typically _____."

- **Simulation** (role play, games, assessment labs): Measures values, style, perceptions by inference based on the trainee's overt behavior in response to posed situations.

- **Multiple-choice situational analysis:** Like the prior example, except that the situations are described on paper instead of enacted live. Also, the range of possible responses is restricted to those given, but each multiple-choice response indicates a different attitude (style, value).

- **Case method:** Measures the extent to which the trainee in analyzing the case agrees or disagrees with the attitudes expressed by the persons depicted in the case. Think of case method as the written equivalent of a projective test.

Evaluating Attitudes: The Challenging One

Although attitude change is more difficult to measure than is the acquisition of knowledge or skill, many new instruments and techniques have evolved in the past few decades—tools that are user-friendly and can be applied to trainees without formal training in psychology or psychometrics. Elements of two such exercises are reprinted on the pages that follow:

Employee Involvement (EI) Status Survey. This instrument measures attitudes toward EI after employees have been trained to function more autonomously in work groups where they participate in problem solving and quality improvement.

Profile of Aptitudes for Leadership (PAL). In organizations that run leadership training and attempt to increase the entrepreneurial spirit (risk taking, envisioning, innovating), this instrument can be used to discern relative strengths among four styles of leadership (manager, supervisor, entrepreneur, technician).

Employee Involvement Status Survey

Directions: For each of the 20 statements that describe the status of employee involvement (EI) in your work situation, indicate the extent to which you agree or disagree by circling the box that best reflects your feelings. Please respond to all 20 questions.

If you agree strongly, circle the box with the two plus signs. If you are inclined to agree, circle the box with the single plus sign. If you feel neutral, circle the box that contains a zero. If you are inclined to disagree, circle the box with the single minus sign. If you disagree strongly, circle the box with the two minus signs.

1. EI has given our employees a way to participate in decisions affecting their work. `++ + 0 - --`

2. Local management pays lip service to EI but has not given the program the active support it needs to succeed. `++ + 0 - --`

3. The use of EI work group meetings to solve problems is growing and finding acceptance at our location. `++ + 0 - --`

4. There is general agreement around here that EI is outmoded and no longer serves its purpose. `++ + 0 - --`

5. Our managers have made significant strides in becoming more participative and more committed to EI. `++ + 0 - --`

6. EI meetings are okay when production and quality are down, but when productivity is up, EI efforts tend to fall off. `++ + 0 - --`

7. Although there have been some setbacks, EI is working at our location. `++ + 0 - --`

8. EI work groups have not received the training needed to enable them to function effectively. `++ + 0 - --`

9. There are many examples of savings in the thousands of dollars resulting from problems solved by EI work groups. `++ + 0 - --`

10. Employees here are disappointed with EI and feel that it is more form than substance. `++ + 0 - --`

11. Participants in our EI work groups are satisfied with the part they play in helping the company to improve. `++ + 0 - --`

12. After their initial training, EI groups are often left on their own with little feedback, recognition, or assistance. `++ + 0 - --`

13. Members of EI problem solving groups look forward to their meetings and the benefits of participating. `++ + 0 - --`

14. EI isn't going to be effective here until the "old guard" of autocratic management retires. `++ + 0 - --`

15. I am sold on the benefits of participating in EI meetings and feel that it is a worthwhile program. `++ + 0 - --`

16. In many EI work group meetings the supervisor is not involved and may not even be present at meetings. `++ + 0 - --`

17. The steering committee at our location has been very helpful in providing support to the EI program. `++ + 0 - --`

18. EI work groups recommend solutions to problems, but often no one takes responsibility for follow-up action. `++ + 0 - --`

19. Both management and the union support EI efforts at our location. `++ + 0 - --`

20. EI is seen by many as a program that is suited for "bad economic times." `++ + 0 - --`

Profile of Aptitude for Leadership (PAL): A Self-Assessment Exercise

Leaders come in a variety of sizes, shapes, and styles. This assessment puts the magnifying glass on leadership style and the ways in which it influences others and accomplish goals, both personal and organizational. Many assessments of style are based on the assumptions we make about employees, the nature of work, and the role of management. They yield scores on such dimensions as the degree to which an employee is Theory X or Theory Y, parent-to-child or adult-to-adult; one who controls others or empowers them; one who prefers dependence or independence in one's associates. This assessment is different. It is designed to help identify preferences among different types of leadership behavior, then explains their implications in order to increase awareness of how leadership styles influence others.

The exercise presents a series of statements that describe the behavior (values, perceptions, actions) of leaders, as seen below. Each set of statements presents four styles of leadership: manager, supervisor, entrepreneur, and technician. Test participants assign points to each set in whatever combination best reflects their agreement with each statement, entering the ratings in the boxes preceding the statements. The scoring results enable participants to identify their leadership preferences.

1. I have a tendency to
   - ❏ be disappointed when people I've instructed don't perform well
   - ❏ focus on problems and work on systems for avoiding them in the future
   - ❏ do things myself and enjoy the satisfaction and closure of a job well done
   - ❏ see opportunities and envision a different and better tomorrow.

2. The road to success in business, as in life, is to assess
   - ❏ and improve use of manpower, methods, machines, materials, and money
   - ❏ the needs of tomorrow's customers and society
   - ❏ the skills of other people, then draw on these skills
   - ❏ and build upon my personal strengths and success as an individual.

3. I would like to have more time to
   - ❏ think about the challenges and situations that lie ahead
   - ❏ do the kinds of work I'm good at but have turned over to other
   - ❏ manage by objectives rather than by fire fighting and crisis
   - ❏ coach people and strengthen my team.

4. The training programs most relevant to my own development deal with
   - ❏ improving personal productivity, avoiding interruptions (time management)
   - ❏ giving on-the-job training, coaching, counseling, disciplining
   - ❏ selling ideas, changing attitudes, thinking creatively
   - ❏ problem solving, management by objectives, methods improvement.

5. I spend a lot of time
   - ❏ working on ideas that may take years to make operational
   - ❏ doing projects that require my technical or professional competence
   - ❏ overseeing systems and procedures to make our work run more smoothly
   - ❏ working with people to improve the quality and quantity of their work.

6. It annoys me when top management
   - ❏ makes changes in direction that disrupt my work mid-stream
   - ❏ views employees as a commodity and doesn't consult them
   - ❏ spends time doing things right instead of doing the right things
   - ❏ fails to give clear objectives and strategies for achieving them.

7. People come to me when they need someone to help them
   - ❏ restore order and impose a system to replace chaos
   - ❏ turn out quality work that others have failed to deliver
   - ❏ improve motivation and productivity among employees
   - ❏ innovate and generate creative approaches to new challenges.

8. One of the things managers often find missing is
   - ❏ a close tie with the supervisors who are their link with employees
   - ❏ long-range vision and a willingness to take risks
   - ❏ the joy of doing work themselves instead of through others
   - ❏ having the right resources at the right times to meet their goals.

9. I get a lot of satisfaction from
   - ❏ planning ways to help others work better and smarter
   - ❏ turning out quality work without anyone breathing down my neck
   - ❏ dreaming up new products or services
   - ❏ fostering teamwork and commitment.

10. We'd be in better shape today if we spent more time
    ❑ doing actual work instead of planning, analyzing, and thinking about work
    ❑ finding out what customers need and expect in the years ahead
    ❑ preparing our employees to deliver their very best
    ❑ improving our systems and procedures—the very ways we do business.

11. Among my real strengths is my ability to
    ❑ think up different things we should be doing down the road
    ❑ impart my skills and abilities to others
    ❑ develop ways of ensuring quality output in meeting our goals
    ❑ turn out demanding work better than my supervisor can.

12. I'm very concerned that
    ❑ our employees receive the best supervision we can give them
    ❑ find ways of working smarter rather than harder
    ❑ we not kill off initiative by becoming overly organized
    ❑ the future not be a repeat of the past.

Four Types of Leadership and Their Characteristics

	M **Manager** (Administrator, Director)	**S** **Supervisor** (Overseer, Coach)
Leadership style	Leads by defining goals and organizing systems and resources for achieving them	Leads by coaching, motivating, and rewarding others to perform
Looks for	Ways to get the best "input mix" of manpower, methods, machines, materials, and money so as to produce the desired output as cost-effectively as possible	Identifying and eliminating problems that keep employees from getting the work out
Places high value on	Conformity, order, control, paperwork, systems, accountability	Loyalty, teamwork, self-discipline, commitment, cooperation
Driven by a desire for	Fail-safe systems and procedures, stability	Motivated employees and teamwork
Creates conditions for	Lower risk, predictability	Job satisfaction for employees
Time frame	Present, strongly influenced by past: "We've always done it this way," or "We've never done anything like that before."	Present: "Here's how we're going to do it," or "How can we best meet our goals?"
Negative consequences	Bureaucracy, paralysis by analysis, unnecessary rules and regulations and paperwork	Under pressure may revert to doing the work instead of getting work done through others
Slogan	"Getting things done smarter rather than harder" (Doing things right)	"Getting things done through others" (Doing everything through teamwork)
Orientation	Inward/outward—a balance of the right input mix to achieve the desired outputs (the management cycle)	Outward, oriented toward producing products and services at predetermined levels of quantity and quality
Proactive/ reactive/Active	Proactive and reactive	Reactive

	E Entrepreneur (Visionary, Leader)	**T** Technician (Specialist, Professional)
Leadership style	Leads by providing a vision of how things might be in the future	Leads by example and personal experience in chosen field of expertise
Looks for	Opportunities that haven't been seen or realized to their fullest; ways to make life easier or the world a better place	More time and fewer interruptions and crises so as to devote full energies to the work at hand
Places high value on	Self-realization, inspiration, striving, change	Personal ability and individual excellence
Driven by a desire for	Ideas, change, innovation, excitement	Freedom to apply one's talent without hassle from others
Creates conditions for	High risk, flux, uncertainty	Job satisfaction for self; control of one's destiny
Time frame	Future, influenced by the imperfect present: "What if we were to...," or "I've got an idea as to how we might...."	Present: "There's work to be done; let's stop talking and get it done," or "How can we ever get all this work done?"
Negative consequences	Threat to stability of organization and job security of employees	Does it all personally; becomes bottle-neck; organization becomes too dependent; the indispensable person
Slogan	"Getting things done right is not as important as getting the right things done." (Doing the right things)	"Getting everything done—if you want a job done right, do it yourself." (Doing everything personally)
Orientation	Outward, oriented toward customers and their future needs and present frustrations with things as they are	Inward, using best inputs of which one is capable; primarily personal energy and expertise
Proactive/ reactive/Active	Proactive	Active

Interpreting the Results

After completing the text, participants realize that there are very few statements with which they strongly disagree. Rather, it is the extent of agreement with each that reflects a style of leadership. They also realize that there is no such thing as one monolithic style of leadership. Rather, we are a combination of many styles, some stronger than others.

Leadership requires the use of power, to influence the thoughts and actions of other people. And power in the hands of an individual entails risk. In the past decade or so, organizations have fostered a new power ethic that favors collective leadership over the individual exercise of power. Teamwork and group decision making are replacing the "personality theory" of leadership. There are many benefits to employee involvement and participative management: better commitment, a balance of power, shared risk, improved productivity. However, the organization may suffer losses in imagination (vision, creativity, innovation), speed of execution, and the danger of "group think" (the so-called Abilene paradox).

Central to any discussion of the uses and distribution of power is the issue of source. Where does power come from? Must it be conferred from an outside source? Does it come from within a leader? And, if so, is it hereditary or can it be developed? (An amazing amount of verbiage has been written in support of each of these views of leadership.)

If we accept the fact that humans are successful (at work, play, family) to the degree that they are effective in influencing the thoughts and actions of others, then we are all leaders. And everyday use of the term *leadership* supports this. Indeed, the only person who is not a leader is the person who has no followers or dependents—a hermit, or a sole survivor. A more restrictive definition of leadership is appropriate in examining organizational behavior, however. We've identified four types of leadership, and described the characteristics of each in the pages that follow.

The Manager/Administrator as Leader

Managers exist to provide order and organization. Within each of us is the person who saves boxes or jars so as to store and label our worldly goods. Perhaps it's nuts and bolts, nails and screws, or hobby parts. Perhaps its buttons or jewelry or kitchen spices in matched bottles. The manager in each of us hangs our tools (lawn, carpentry, cooking) in impeccable order on the wall.

Managers are a product of past conditioning. They crave order and the security of the status quo. They sometimes view change as a threat—a source of potential problems and a disruption to their orderly system. They see entrepreneurs as intruders who jeopardize the neat systems they've installed. They see supervisors as their sergeants and lieutenants who can muster the troops to carry out the policies and procedures that are essential to maintaining order, predictability, and accountability. And they see technicians as one component, the "human" resource, in the array of resources they manage (manpower, methods, materials, machines, money—the five Ms of management).

The manager thrives on imposing or maintaining systems so that each operation is effective, highly predictable, controllable, efficient. This is done through planning, scheduling, directing, and controlling—the four stages of the management cycle.

The Supervisor/Coach as Leader

Supervisors fill a leadership role that is sometimes boss (parent-to-child) and sometimes coach (adult-to-adult), getting work done through others. They see the members of their team as, alternately, winners and losers. They move from pride and elation ("I've got the best people in the whole organization—great job, gang!") to disappointment and annoyance ("I knew I should have done it myself—you guys really blew it!").

We are all on the continuum that stretches between the two extremes identified by Douglas McGregor as Theory X and Theory Y. We see it in supervising our children, our friends, our fellow employees. Sometimes our children can do no wrong (after all, they are our children). Sometimes they can do no right ("What do I have to do to get you to...").

Supervisors crave teamwork: cooperation, consensus, commitment. In filling their role as coach, they rely on goal setting (motivation), training, counseling, delegating, disciplining, and rewarding (reinforcement). Supervisors see managers as bosses and themselves as coaches. Managers determine strategies, while supervisors deal with tactics. Managers are sometimes seen as inhumane ("They have no appreciation for my people—no understanding of human feelings."). Supervisors see entrepreneurs as agents of change and disruptive to productivity and commitment. And they see technicians as loners and mavericks who don't know the meaning of teamwork and cooperation.

The Entrepreneur/Visionary as Leader

Entrepreneurs see things not as they are but as they might be. Everyday conditions challenge and spark these people to make them better: to see innovation, to experiment, to be a catalyst for change. Entrepreneurs live in the future, a world of overabundant opportunities. We find entrepreneurs in every field: science (Albert Einstein, Thomas Edison), art (Van Gogh, Matisse), business (Henry Ford, Ray Kroc of McDonald's).

There is an entrepreneur within each of us—our creative side, converting matter into art, prodding the unknown, and shaping our future. The entrepreneur within us creates havoc and unrest in those around us. As they fall behind or feel outdistanced, we require more and more effort to pull our colleagues along, or even to get them to understand and accept what we're trying to do. The entrepreneur's world is the conflict between boundless opportunities and people who don't share the vision and won't climb on board.

Because entrepreneurs thrive on change, they see managers and supervisors as clinging to the status quo, conjuring up problems ("We've never done anything like that before—I don't know.") instead of seeing opportunities. Similarly, entrepreneurs see technicians as the ones who can get things done and execute the changes they envision.

The Technician/Specialist as Leader

Technicians are their own master. They work best alone because they are happiest when applying their talents to the work at hand. They work steadily and dependably, one thing at a time, and have a need to control the work at hand.

To the technician, thinking and dreaming are unproductive. The how-to-do-it right now is more important than planning for a new tomorrow or generating more efficient methods for today. This leads the technician to distrust managers, supervisors, and entrepreneurs, all of whom are a disruption to work ("They see me as just another cog in their machine—their dehumanized system. The best way to get work done correctly and efficiently is to do it yourself.") Your dentist, lawyer, accountant, TV repairman, and auto mechanic are probably technicians. So are the majority of artists, musicians, and writers. So are the people in the computer room, the quality control lab, and the advertising department.

Like the entrepreneur, the technician is very difficult to manage. They are most productive when left alone and managed at a distance. Technicians are not leaders in the usual sense of having a loyal band of followers. (Neither are managers or entrepreneurs, for that matter.) But they are respected and depended upon by many others. They own the stores and restaurants on Main Street, USA. They provide professional services to a society that requires quality and expertise. They are leaders in their profession.

In summary

The Profile of Aptitude for Leadership (PAL) identifies four styles of leadership. Each is appropriate in different situations. All are essential to the smooth functioning of a society (nation, community, organization). All four styles are present to a greater or lesser degree in each of us, shaped by our heredity and environment.

A quick perspective on the four styles might be gained by comparing an organization to a sailing ship. The entrepreneur is the sail, moving the ship into new waters (which can be both exulting and scary for those on board). The manager is the keel, trying to keep the boat stable and upright in uncertain waters. A sailboat without a keel is likely to blow over. A sailboat with keel but no sail is dead in the water. Each needs the other. As for the crew, they include the supervisors and technicians. Supervisors oversee the day-to-day activities that keep the ship sailing, and technicians handle the specialized functions that require professional skills and relatively little supervision: cooking, radio operations, navigation. Many other members of the crew (sailors) are needed to operate a large sailing ship. They are followers, not leaders.

CHAPTER 15

MEASURING SKILLS DEVELOPMENT

Upon completing this chapter you should be able to

◆ state at least three benefits of evaluating skills via simulations and not reality

◆ indicate the weakness of a simulation (that is, what it cannot evaluate)

◆ list at least six tools or techniques for evaluating skills

◆ describe the three components of using script for analysis (Tom and Jim)

◆ select the methods that are most appropriate to evaluate your skills training.

Skills are relatively easy to evaluate—simply get the trainee to perform. If the equipment is inexpensive, readily available, and not likely to interfere with other operations, we can give trainees a batch of work and have them perform it. Examples include operating a drill press, using a PC for word processing, driving a car. Sometimes, however, the three conditions just noted are not present. For example, how would you evaluate if your trainee were a commercial jet pilot, a firefighter, or a nuclear power plant operator? In these cases we resort to simulation, examples of which are shown below.

Actual operations. We observe the trainee performing actual work on the job (or at a workstation that duplicates the situation at work).

Simulations. We simulate as nearly as we can the conditions our trainees will face on the job. Several familiar forms of simulation follow:

Role play. Best for measuring interpersonal skills in courses for salespeople, customer service representatives, supervisors, interviewers, counselors

Case method. Best for measuring skills in problem solving, decision making, analytical thinking, writing and editing

In-basket. Best for measuring skills in organizing, prioritizing, time management, delegating, decision making, problem solving

Lab and bench work. Best for measuring skills in technical areas: troubleshooting, assembly, diagnosing problems on "bugged" equipment

Script analysis. Best for measuring the same skills as noted in role play, only here the trainee critiques and rewrites a scripted interaction

Paper-and-pencil test. Best for measuring skills that normally occur on paper: grammar skills, PERT and CPA for project managers, writing, forms processing

Notice that the first four evaluation techniques are labor intensive and require personal observation by the instructor or other trained observers. Also, the trainee typically expects verbal feedback at the time, in answer to the "How am I doing?" question. In contrast, the last four techniques require written responses from the trainees. As such, they can be evaluated and scored thereafter. Thus, the administration of the instrument is not instructor dependent. The real issue is not one of convenience, however. Rather, it concerns the skills we have taught and whether they can be measured by paper and pencil or whether they require hands-on activity.

The Simulation vs. Reality Trade-off

In evaluating trainees' skills, there is no substitute for reality—for putting them in the workplace and having them handle actual situations. Or is there? Actually, simulation may be a better substitute than reality itself. By simulating the conditions of the workplace, we gain many advantages that are important to successful evaluation.

- ◆ We have control over the stimuli (situations, problems, opportunities) we want the trainee to respond to. We have little or no control over the daily work flow and the situations that might arise when we place a person in the workplace and evaluate their performance on the job.

- ◆ We can compress time and thereby have more stimuli per unit of time. Days might be required to observe workplace behavior and capture a diverse set of skills that can be observed in an hour or so of simulated experience.

- ◆ Mistakes aren't fatal in a simulation. We can protect the trainees, fellow employees, or customers from the consequences of inappropriate behavior. This is often not possible in real situations.

- ◆ The simulation is ready when we are ready to assess. There is no need to make special arrangements to place the trainee in the workplace, involving supervisors, fellow employees, or transportation).

- ◆ All trainees can be evaluated against the same stimuli since they are all responding to the same conditions. We can control the uniformity of the situations that we design into the simulation. Ratings are thus seen as much fairer.

These are the advantages of simulating reality. But there are trade-off. What we lose, of course, is the opportunity to see how our learners will respond to the daily interruptions, barriers, and constraints that are a very real part of the workplace environment. So we must accept the fact that a simulation can evaluate whether our trainees have learned and can apply their new learning, but we can not evaluate whether they will apply their new skills under adverse conditions in the workplace.

The pages that follow contain an example of an assessment used to measure skills development. "Tom and Jim" makes use of script analysis to evaluate one's skill in giving on-the-job training. This exercise could also be done as a role play, with the instructor playing the role of Jim and the trainee giving the instruction correctly (after reading the incorrect script and planning how to do it correctly).

Tom and Jim

Tom is a supervisor who is just about to give one of his people, Jim, an assignment to paint some windows in a warehouse. They are up near the ceiling, so Jim is going to have to use an extension ladder. Read this script of the training that Tom gave Jim. Then make notes beside the script to indicate what Tom did wrong or failed to do. Refer to Tom's comments by number to save writing.

Tom: 1 You'll have to use the extension ladder to reach the upper ones, Jim. Do
2 you know how it operates?

Jim: 3 Yeah. I've got an aluminum one at home.

Tom: 4 Good. Set the ladder up so it's leaning against the window sill at the top
5 and out far enough at the bottom to make an angle of about 70 degrees
6 with the ground. You want it extended far enough so that you can always
7 grip the ladder with one hand while painting with the other. Never stand
8 on the top or next to the top rung. If you have to go that high, come back
9 down and extend the ladder farther up. Understand?

Jim: 10 Yeah.

Tom: 11 Okay. Let's make sure. Can you name the three things to remember
12 when using an extension ladder?

Jim: 13 Let's see. Extend it far enough so I can hold on to it while painting.

Tom: 14 Good. That's one of 'em.

Jim: 15 Keep the ladder slanted at a 70-degree angle.

Tom: 16 Two down, only one to go.

Jim: 17 And . . . uhh . . . are you sure there was a third?

Tom: 18 Yes. . . the first one. Lean the top of the ladder against the window sill,
19 not against the glass or the thin wood separating the panes.

Jim: 20 Oh, yeah.

Tom: 21 Okay. Once you get up there, what will you paint first?

Jim: 22 The thin wood strips that separate the panes.

Tom: 23 Nope. Start with the parts of the window that are farthest away from 24 you, then work your way in toward you. A good rule to follow is to 25 paint the part that is hardest to get to first, and then end up with the 26 parts that show the most. If you are painting a chair or stool, first do the 27 underside and the insides of the legs. The last things to paint are the 28 fronts of the legs and the seat. Do you think you understand?

Jim: 29 Yeah. I think so.

Tom: 30 Then go to it. You know where I'll be if you have any problems. I'll 31 check back in about a half-hour to see how things are going.

Jim: 32 Okay. I shouldn't have any trouble.

A critique of this script analysis. Here are 12 failures we spotted—situations where Tom specifically failed to apply one or more of the learning principles we've been discussing. Go back and check your own evaluation of Tom, and see how many of these failures you were able to identify.

1. At the very start, Tom should have begun the instruction by explaining what Jim would be able to do when the instruction was over (the terminal behavior): "Jim, you'll be painting the windows today, so I'd like to take five minutes to make sure you know how to operate the extension ladder and how to paint the thin strips that separate the panes."

2. In line 4, Tom seemed to ignore Jim's response to the question, "Do you know how it operates?" Having one at home is not the same as knowing how it operates. Tom should have asked Jim to set up the ladder and **demonstrate** his understanding of how it operates.

3. In lines 4-9, Tom gives out a lot of information without checking to see if Jim understands. There are three different pieces of information in this paragraph—three **stimuli.** Tom should have stopped after each one to get a relevant **response** from Jim and thereby make sure he understands.

4. In line 5, Tom has no idea whether or not Jim can visualize a 70-degree angle. Is he carrying a protractor with him? It would have been better if Tom had asked Jim to show him what a safe angle would be by leaning the ladder against the wall. He could then find out if Jim understands what a safe angle really means.

5. In line 9, "Understand?" is a poor question. Jim is likely to answer Yes whether or not he understands. In fact he may not even **know** whether or not he understands. In other words, the question does not elicit a relevant response, since (a) trainees often can't tell whether or not they understand, and (b) even if they don't understand they may not want to say so to their instructor for fear of offending or of looking dumb.

6. In line 11, Tom asks Jim to name the three things to remember. Naming them is not the same as doing them. Again, Tom is wasting time. He should have gotten Jim to **do** the three things, and watched him while he did so. Many people are not verbal and are a lot more comfortable doing things than talking about them.

7. In lines 18-19, Tom should explain why he's giving these instructions. Or, it might be better if Tom had asked, "Jim, could you tell me **why** you'd lean the ladder against the upper sill rather than the lower?" Tom could then find out if Jim understands ladder placement: It can only go against the upper sill, and not against the lower sill, the panes, or the wood between them.

8. In line 21, this would normally be a good question. It is trainee centered, and shows that Tom wants to find out what Jim already knows before teaching him. Given Tom's style of instruction up to this point, however, such a question probably looks like a test to Jim—a test of something he hasn't been taught yet. As such, it is likely to put Jim on the spot. He may be thinking, "Tom must have covered this, but I don't remember it." In short, your style as instructor should be consistent. Switching from the information-centered style to a trainee-centered one may confuse the trainee.

9. In line 23, having just tried to find out what Jim already knows, Tom's "Nope" sounds something like "Gotcha, you idiot!" It almost looks as if Tom had tried to set Jim up and to trap him. Instead, Tom should have led Jim on and helped him to see the adverse results of painting the thin wood strips first. Tom forgot our first principle: We learn best, not by being told, but by experiencing the consequences of our actions.

10. In line 26, right after saying, "Then end up with the parts that show the most," Tom should have thrown the ball to Jim, asking him: "Now Jim, let's see if you understand. Suppose you were going to paint a chair. How would you go about it? What parts would you paint first?" Any time you have to teach a rule or principle or procedure, it's a good idea to get the trainee to describe an example of it. This is one of the best ways to get feedback and thus complete the stimulus-response-feedback link.

11. In line 28, look at the question, "Do you think you understand?" Again, this question is a poor one, since it is likely to get an irrelevant response. How does Jim know if he really understands until he does it? (Same problem here as the one we discussed in no. 5.)

12. In line 30, Tom ends up with, "You know where I'll be if you run into any problems." That's bad. He should remain long enough to check Jim out and give him feedback. By so doing, he can correct poor techniques and reinforce good ones at the start. In the application stage of our learning model, the instructor should watch the learner **apply** what has just been acquired. This is the only way to find out if the instruction has been successful.

The Desired Behavior. Now let's rewrite the script, using the information we have gleaned from our critique.

Tom: You'll have to use the extension ladder on the upper ones, Jim. Do you know how it operates?

Jim: Yeah. I've got an aluminum one at home.

Tom: Good. Well, let's use this one right here. Why don't you show me where you'd place it to paint that window up there? In other words, show me a safe angle for the ladder.

Jim: Okay. (He sets ladder against window sill.) How's this?

Tom: Looks good. What will happen if you pull the base out farther away from the wall?

Jim: The base might begin to slip and shoot out from under me.

Tom: And how about the opposite direction? What if you move the base closer to the wall?

Jim: Then the ladder will be too upright. If I lean back, it could go over backwards.

Tom: Good. I notice that you have the ladder resting on the bottom window sill.

Jim: Yeah. If I put it higher, it will be resting on the glass or the thin framing between the panes. And they're not strong enough.

Tom: True. But how are you going to reach the top of the window?

Jim: I can stand on the top rung of the ladder.

Tom: That's a bit dangerous, isn't it? A safer way to reach the top is to extend the ladder farther up so that it rests on the wall above the window. Why is this safer, Jim?

Jim: Uhh ... because I can hold on to the ladder with one hand while I'm painting with the other.

Tom: Exactly. Now, once you get up there, what are you going to do? What will you paint first?

Jim: The thin wood strips that separate the panes.

Tom: Why are you starting with these?

Jim: Because they are the easiest to reach.

Tom: Yeah, but what's going to happen as you reach out to paint the sides of the window frame and the parts that are harder to reach? You may get your sleeve in the fresh paint.

Jim: Okay, then I guess it would be better if I start by painting the parts that are farthest away and work my way in.

Tom: Much better idea. In fact, that's a good rule to follow, whatever you're painting: First paint the part that's hardest to get to; then end up with the parts that show the most. So if you are painting a chair or stool, where would you start?

Jim: Uhh ... the underside. And the inside of the legs.

Tom: What part would you save 'til last?

Jim: The fronts of the legs and the seat.

Tom: Good. I can see that you understand. So, go to it. I'll be at my desk if you run into any problems. But I'll check back in a half-hour or so to see how things are going.

Jim: Okay. I shouldn't have any trouble.

CHAPTER 16

COMPETENCY-BASED ASSESSMENT

Upon completing this chapter you should be able to

◆ define what is meant by a competency

◆ explain why the trend is toward competency-based training

◆ state why a three-legged stool is a good symbol for course content

◆ give an example of the difference between a competency and a skill.

The last three chapters have dealt with knowledge, attitudes, and skills (KAS) as independent variables that influence our behavior. In some courses they are, and can be evaluated separately. However, in many types of training the three are integrally linked and should be taught—and evaluated—in a unified manner.

Competency-based training and the assessment of competency are terms used increasingly by trainers to refer to the interaction of the three variables. Each is strongly influenced by the other two, and trainees will learn and perform most effectively when the three are taught and evaluated as an overlay and not as separate domains. The diagram illustrates this overlay.

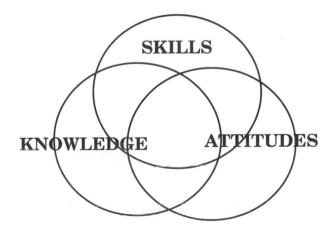

The training of supervisors, managers, salespersons, customer service representatives, and many others is more effective when based on competencies rather than on skills only (how-to-do-it) or knowledge only (policy, procedures, principles) or attitudes only (feelings, beliefs, values). Moreover, participants find competency-based instruction more relevant than the fragmented design found in many courses.

Let's take an example. Time management is needed in all the jobs just listed. It's usually taught as a skill—a series of how-to-do-it guidelines (how to delegate, prioritize, keep a "to do" list, negotiate, say No tactfully, deal with interruptions). Such courses often have little permanent impact other than increasing one's realization that time management is important, difficult, and not handled very effectively on either an individual or organizational basis. Why is this so? Because time management is a competency, not a skill. The knowledge side (Do you know the actual cost of an hour of your time, or of those with whom you work?) and the attitude side (Are you willing to negotiate or say No to your boss or a key client?) are essential ingredients to the effective instruction and evaluation of this competency.

Until recently, assessment labs were the primary means of evaluating competencies. But advances in technology (computers, interactive video) now make it possible to develop exercises to evaluate competencies in a much more user-friendly manner than the assessment labs of yesterday. The following pages contain a discussion of the trend toward competency-based training. Several examples illustrate the difference between competencies and skills, and point to the greater return-on-investment of the training dollar when we equip trainees with competencies that go beyond skills. Perhaps the best examples of competency-based training are found in the areas of management development, customer service, and sales training. Any instrument used to evaluate competencies (assessment lab, video-based simulation, psychological tests) should be validated via a correlation analysis to ensure its validity.

The Trend Toward Competency-Based Training

What is a competency? Human behavior in the workplace (or anywhere else, for that matter) is shaped by what you know, how you feel, and what you can do: knowledge, attitudes, and skills. Picture these as a three-legged stool: If any leg is missing, you won't get the desired performance.

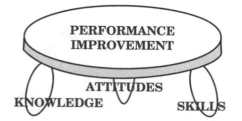

A competency is defined as a cluster of related KAS working together to produce outstanding performance in a given area of responsibility (for example, time management, analytical thinking, getting unbiased information). Competency-based training recognizes that all three factors must be addressed and taught in an integrated manner. To be sure, there are many factors in the workplace that also affect human performance, but our discussion is limited to those factors we can assess (to determine need) and teach (to improve performance). Let's agree to call these factors competencies.

A brief look (and gross oversimplification) of the history of human resources development might be useful. In the beginning, courses emphasized knowledge—lots of facts, theory, concepts. Training manuals were crammed with information, and classes were heavy on lectures, supplemented by slides, overheads, and handouts. Then we saw an increased emphasis on attitudes: sensitivity training, outward-bound programs (team building, survival), assertiveness, awareness, human relations, and motivation. Next came a shift to the hard-nosed, no-nonsense emphasis on skills: how-to-do-it programs, behavior modeling, simulations, role play, and more hands-on learning.

Soon we began to realize that each of these approaches is limited. An integration of KAS provides a more nourishing menu for trainees. Competency studies also showed us the folly of looking at the legs of our stool as separate, isolated support: All three must work together. Moreover, there's a dependency relationship among the three factors that is illustrated by the model. Think of the triangle as an iceberg. Skills are the tip of the iceberg, the part above the surface. (We can see skills as overt behavior; knowledge and attitudes lie beneath the surface.)

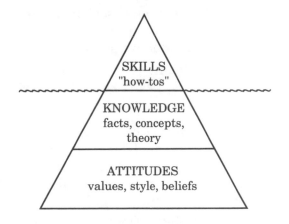

We are quick to judge people based on their skills, since they are so visible. Yet the presence or absence of skills in a person is heavily dependent on knowledge—the facts, concepts, principles, theory, policy, and procedures that serve as the foundation for skills development. And the knowledge we choose to accept or reject (retain or forget, seek or avoid) is, in turn, strongly influenced by our attitudes—the values, beliefs, styles, perceptions, and opinions that make us who we are. Hence the hierarchy shown in our iceberg model.

An Example: Time Management

Let's examine a typical course to illustrate our iceberg model: time management. This topic is usually taught as a skill rather than a competency: how to prioritize, delegate, make up "to do" lists, negotiate to upgrade and downgrade. In many organizations now using a skills-based approach to time management, the transfer of training from workshop to workplace is minimal. Participants quickly revert to old habits and management by crisis (or management by the latest "opportunity du jour," which quickly leads to management by crisis!)

A competency-based approach recognizes that it's the absence of knowledge and attitudes (values, perceptions) rather than skills that keeps us from managing our time more effectively. Few people realize that the actual cost of an hour of their time to the organization is close to $100 per hour for a $50,000-per-year employee. Course participants can calculate their actual cost, as well as their productivity ratio: how many actual hours per day were devoted to accomplishing their goals and standards. This is important knowledge that's missing from most skills-based courses.

Now let's go to the base level of our iceberg and examine attitudes. Here are some of the perceptions and values of a typical action-oriented manager that interfere with effective time management:

◆ It's forbidden for me to refuse or to renegotiate an assignment from my boss (client, user department).

◆ Management by crisis is much more exciting and challenging than management by objectives.

◆ I'm basically a firefighter, here to help others with their problems. I'm often better and safer in the reactive mode than the proactive.

◆ I'll be seen as self-important if I don't take every phone call, visitor, or meeting and rude if I try to speed up or end an unproductive session.

◆ I'm being paid to spend time (rather than invest it); if I log the hours, I can't be faulted. Everything will get done sooner or later.

Such attitudes can be modified in class through case method, simulations, time log analysis, and other forms of hands-on learning, provided we follow an integrated KAS approach. To be sure, a skills-only approach is less likely to penetrate and annoy a participant with increased self-awareness and the recognition that some closely held values and perceptions are counter-productive. But by the same token, skills-based courses are less likely to change behavior: a one-legged stool is very unstable!

Competencies vs. Skills

Skills-based training often teaches procedures, techniques, and the how-to-do-it aspects of a job without getting beneath the surface of our iceberg model, without addressing cognitive or affective factors that make the difference between superficial performance and excellence. Trainees are a combination of KAS; what they know and how they feel are as important a part of their being as what they can do, and strongly influence what they will do.

There's another difference. Many skills are situational and specific: how to do a selection interview, conduct a performance appraisal, or counsel a problem employee. Courses designed to teach these situational skills often spell out the specific procedure ("action steps" or "key learning points") to be followed. Unfortunately these do not have high potential for transfer of training to other interpersonal situations for which we want our trainees prepared. In addition, the amount of time a supervisor spends doing selection interviews, performance appraisals, and counseling sessions is relatively small, adding up to a half-dozen hours per year.

In contrast, if we teach generic and universal competencies that are the foundation of interpersonal communications (listening, giving clear information, getting unbiased information, using questions effectively, logic and analytical thinking), our courses will have much higher application to the 87% of a typical manager's day that is spent interacting with others. We'll have upgraded their effectiveness in all human interactions, not just in interviews and appraisals. To be sure, we can use these specific situations (and others) as the settings for role plays, case studies, scripts for analysis, and simulations. However, they are serving as a means for practicing and refining competencies, and not as the ends for learning specific situational skills.

Let's examine a third feature of competency-based instruction—its relevancy to a broad, heterogeneous audience. Courses for supervisors, managers, salespersons, or instructors often face "mission impossible": to be relevant in the great variety of organizational settings from which participants are drawn. A warehouse supervisor, an information systems supervisor, and a customer service supervisor may have little in common on their specific job skills. But they all need the same competencies of problem solving, setting performance goals and standards, and getting and giving feedback. Instructors who teach diverse populations have long wished for course designs in which "one size fits all." Competency-based training offers this benefit in the universality of the competencies taught, and thereby gets more mileage out of every training dollar invested.

Advantages of Competencies: A Summary

We've examined three features of competency-based training, and the benefits each of these offers to users:

Competency-based training addresses and integrates all three components of human behavior: knowledge, attitudes, and skills.

- Transfer of training from workshop to workplace is much greater (for example, time management).
- Retention and comprehension are greater. We're dealing with the whole person and not a how-to-do-it robot.
- The ability to overcome negative workplace factors is greater: A three-legged stool is stable.

Competencies are generic and universal, serving as the foundation of a broad spectrum of specific skills.

◆ Needs assessment on both an organizational and individual basis is easier with competencies than with K or A or S alone.

◆ Participants find it easier to develop action plans that translate competencies into specific behaviors for their jobs.

◆ There is greater return on investment. Management gets more mileage for every training dollar invested in competency-based training.

Competencies cut across organizational lines and are relevant to many audiences (one size fits all).

◆ Content is applicable in many settings: sales, manufacturing, service, administrative, research and development, regions and headquarters.

◆ All levels of management can sing from the same songbook: supervisors, middle management, executives, technical professionals.

◆ Courses promote team building and a common culture where everyone speaks the same language of competencies.

Given these benefits, it is easy to understand why organizations are turning increasingly to (a) assessment of the competencies needed by trainees to perform their jobs with excellence, and (b) delivery of competency-based modules of instruction that provide a high return on the training investment.

CHAPTER 17

EVALUATING WORKPLACE BEHAVIOR

Upon completing this chapter you should be able to

◆ give at least three examples of courses where pretraining data exists

◆ identify at least three sources (types) of hard data on performance

◆ describe several kinds of forms used to collect posttraining performance

◆ explain what is meant by a shopper's survey.

◆ list at least three courses where graduates use critique sheets on themselves.

Measurements of the impact of training at Level 1 (Did they **like** it?) and Level 2 (Did they **learn** it?) are useful in providing data that can help us to revise and fine-tune our training. But the real payoff of any course can be measured only at Level 3 (Did they **apply** it?). And this means collecting data in the workplace.

Sometimes we can gather hard data to evaluate the impact of a course: sales increased, accidents declined, productivity improved, scrap and rejects reduced. In these examples, existing data (pretraining performance) can be compared with data collected later (posttraining performance) to measure the gain attributable to training. At other times, no record of prior performance exists. We might want to create one in order to compare performance before and after training. For example, in a writing skills course, we can survey our graduates a month after training and request two examples of their correspondence written before and after the course (which we'll then evaluate against the criteria that were our course objectives). Or in a course for supervisors on performance appraisals, we might examine the forms filed with the personnel department on three pretraining appraisals and three posttraining appraisals that each graduate conducted.

In the prior two examples, the results of training are reflected in documents that are tangible and therefore measurable (written correspondence and appraisal forms, both of which exist in files). But what if the training focused on behavior that is interpersonal (retail selling, bank teller training) or manual (machine operations)?

In cases where no documentation of performance exists, we may have to collect hard data either by direct observation in the workplace or by some less obtrusive means such as shopper's surveys, simulations, or hidden cameras. (If you're bothered by hidden cameras or the notion that employees don't know they are being observed, then tell them during training that (a) such measures will be taken, and that (b) their names will not be attached to the performance. Incidentally, this does not preclude giving them feedback. Let's summarize the four sources of hard data:

◆ records already on file that enable us to compare pretraining and posttraining performance, either by individual or on an organizational basis

◆ documents on file that can be evaluated against performance criteria (course objectives) to extract pretraining and posttraining data

◆ direct observation of performance at work (obtrusive data collection) by either the immediate supervisor or a trained observer (for example, the instructor)

◆ direct observation of performance at work (unobtrusive data collection) via shopper's surveys or other covert methods.

The Elusive Levels 3 and 4

The evaluation techniques discussed so far apply to Levels 1 and 2, and can be carried out in class. When we move to Levels 3 and 4, we must go into the workplace to measure performance and results. This is always a challenge for trainers. However, many courses deal with specific behaviors that must occur on the job and that we can observe, either directly or through hard data that is already being collected.

There are a number of forms that can be used to collect data by observing employees back on the job after training. Among them are the following: customer-teller relations rating sheets (used in shopper's surveys of bank tellers and completed by the shopper after each transaction); rating sheets (used to evaluate presentations of recent graduates); a survey of the trade form (used by supervisors and trainers who visit selected outlets following a course on merchandising and space management); a shipping department checklist (used to do spot-checks following training of the shipping department staff); meeting announcement or agenda forms (distributed during a workshop for participants to use in planning and announcing future meetings). On the following pages, we have included samples of two of these forms.

Commercial Bank—Customer-Teller Relations

RATING SHEET

Rating the Teller on Courtesy Toward the Customer

1. Did the teller appear neat, clean, and well groomed? Yes____ No____

2. Did the teller greet the customer with a smile and say good morning (or good afternoon) and use the customer's name? Yes____ No____

3. Did the teller mention something of special interest to the customer? ("Did you have a nice weekend, Mrs. Jones?") Yes____ No____

4. Did the teller say "Excuse me, please" when leaving the customer? (to check a balance or signature) Yes____ No____ N/A____

5. Upon returning to the customer, did the teller say "Sorry to have kept you waiting"? Yes____ No____ N/A____

6. If the teller was busy when the customer reached the window, did the teller say "Excuse me, please, I'll be with you in a moment"? Yes____ No____ N/A____

7. Did the teller assist a disorganized customer by showing the advantages of following the bank's procedures? Yes____ No____ N/A____

8. Did the teller let the customer tell his or her story without being interrupted? Yes____ No____

9. If the customer had a problem that could not be solved by the teller, did the teller refer the customer to a specific person who could be of assistance? Yes____ No____ N/A____

10. When the customer left the window, did the teller say "Good-bye" and "Thank you" and use the customer's name? Yes____ No____

Rating the Teller on Cross-Selling

11. Did the teller recommend any additional bank services to the customer? Yes____ No____

12. Did the teller describe the features of the service to the customer? Yes____ No____

13. Did the teller point out how the customer could benefit from the additional service? Yes____ No____

14. Did the teller refer customer to an officer or platform assistant? Yes_____ No_____

15. Did the teller signal the guard and have him take the customer to a specific person on the platform? Yes_____ No_____

Scoring the Teller's Performance

1. *Courtesy:* Total the number of Yes, No and N/A (not applicable) items related to courtesy toward the customer ____Yes ____No ____N/A.

   Give 5 points for every Yes answer and 2 points for every N/A item.

   (N/A points may be given only for questions 4, 5, 6, 7, and 9 if the behavior could not occur during the transaction.)   Total Courtesy_____

2. *Cross-Selling:* Total the number of Yes and No items.

   Total: ____Yes ____No

   Give 10 points for every Yes answer.   Total Cross-Selling_____

3. Total the points for courtesy and cross-selling.   Customer-Teller Total_____

   A score of 85 or above = excellent

   75 to 84 = good

   65 to 74 = fair

   below 65 = poor customer-teller relations

RATING SHEET

What kind of job did the presenter do in:

		Excel-lent	Very Good	Good	Fair
OPENING	1. Defining the need and the objective clearly in opening statements 2. Presenting objective in terms of how it would benefit the other person				
PRESENTING	3. Establishing a friendly climate 4. Presenting one idea at a time, using evidence or an example to bring it to life 5. Stating the facts and features (especially dollars) as benefits 6. Giving costs of not doing it (if appropriate)* 7. Empathizing by relating to the other person's interests 8. Involving the other person(s) by asking questions 9. Listening attentively 10. Giving feedback to show understanding				
HANDLING OBJECTIONS	11. Re-stating benefits 12. Probing with questions to get real reason for objection (if appropriate)* 13. Using questions to clarify buyer's concerns 14. Referring to past success (sale) or experience (if appropriate)*				
ACTIONS	15. Giving an outline for implementation, explaining who will do what, and when 16. Outlining plans for follow-up, with whom, what, when				
CLOSING	17. Asking appropriate questions to get commitment or desired action 18. Re-stating advantages and disadvantages 19. Soliciting other person's opinion for solution (if appropriate)* 20. Seeking a course of action that was beneficial to both parties				
	Total number of checks				
	Multiply by	4	3	2	1
	To get				

Directions for scoring:

Allow four points for every check mark in the "Excellent" column, three points for every "Very Good," two points for "Good," and one point for "Fair" checks. Thus, a perfect score would be 80 points.

*If these steps are not appropriate, award the presenter an "Excellent."

CHAPTER 18

MEASURING TRANSFER OF SOFT SKILLS

Upon completing this chapter you should be able to

◆ distinguish between soft skills and hard skills, using examples

◆ describe how action plans can be used to improve transfer

◆ list the major parts of an action plan

◆ state four benefits of reviewing action plans as each class session begins

◆ indicate several things trainees should do with their action plans.

In the last chapter, we dealt with hard data on actual performance. Great if you can get it! But some courses deal with performance improvement that is much harder to see and measure in the workplace. In these cases, we must settle for opinions and estimates of perceived improvement (soft data). Here are some examples:

◆ Interpersonal skills that are too personal for us to observe, and where an observer's presence would contaminate (bias) the interaction: selection interviewing, counseling an employee, selling to a problem customer, performance appraisal.

◆ Cognitive skills that take place within the mind and may not have an immediately observable component that we could evaluate: problem solving, decision making, analytical thinking, visualizing, creative thinking, values adjustment.

◆ Infrequent skills that rarely if ever take place: military training for combat, emergency procedures (fire, police, medics, aircraft, nuclear power plant operations), crisis management (sabotage, contamination of product, kidnapping of CEO).

If we cannot get hard data on actual performance (for reasons like those shown above), then we can get soft data on actual performance (opinions of perceived improvement), or we might get hard data on simulations of work conditions (which we can observe). In collecting soft data (opinions) on actual performance, we usually rely on interviews or surveys conducted with trainees and those who know their performance (supervisors, customers, subordinates, with their permission, of course). In collecting hard data (factual) on the trainee's performance in simulations (role plays, assessment labs, in-basket, open-ended case method), we usually rely on direct observation by trained observers.

Action Plans and Individual Development Plans

End-of-course evaluations should measure more than learning. The commitment of trainees to apply new learning is equally important, as is the commitment of their managers to follow up by recognizing and reinforcing their new behaviors back on the job. Two tools that enable us to evaluate and strengthen commitment are the action plan and the individual development plan. Trainers can follow up a month or so after a training program is over to see the degree to which the actions spelled out by participants and agreed to by their supervisors have been carried out at work, and with what results.

An action plan is probably the most useful tool for affixing the responsibility for performance and its evaluation on trainees and their managers. Some of the actions that trainees resolve to take (actual performance) can be evaluated by collecting hard data, while other actions are (a) interpersonal or (b) cognitive in nature and will require soft data evaluations by self, manager, or other "stakeholders." Thus, the action plan is a tool that helps to resolve the actual vs. perceived dilemma—it applies to both.

On the following pages you will find (a) a set of instructions designed to prepare trainers to introduce participants to the use of action plans to facilitate the transfer of training (includes a sample four-page action plan); and (b) an individual development plan to be completed by trainers and shared with their managers. In these examples, the evaluation of a program's effectiveness is based on (a) the degree to which the plans were implemented, and (b) the observations by supervisors of performance improvement in those areas that both parties agreed to work on as spelled out in the plan.

Using Action Plans for Transfer of Training

We view participants not as empty vessels waiting to attend class and be filled with new concepts and skills, but rather as "change agents" and catalysts who are being equipped with tools and techniques that they will apply back on the job. The vehicle for accomplishing this is the action plan. It's a form that each participant completes at the end of each workshop session. Think of it as a "transmittal document" that participants take back to their managers and their work group, discussing it and agreeing on how new tools and techniques acquired in class can be transplanted and put into action on the job.

Since participants need time between workshop sessions to refine, discuss, and begin to implement their action plan, we recommend that course sessions be scheduled one to two weeks apart. (This is not possible, of course, when people must travel and be put up overnight.) At the start of each new workshop, participants get out their action plans and discuss the results of their meetings with managers and work group, working in subgroups of three to four persons each. These action plan reviews serve several useful purposes:

- They provide continuity to the course by reviewing the prior session's content.
- They place emphasis on applying concepts and skills, not merely acquiring them.
- They give you feedback on where participants need help in putting skills into practice.
- They enable you to follow up with managers who aren't meeting with participants.
- They reinforce participants for investing the extra time needed outside class.
- They give you a meaningful means of measuring the impact of the course.

Action plans are appropriate whether or not your participants are sharing them with their managers between the training sessions. The impact is far greater, however, when each participant's manager becomes a partner in their development. This is best accomplished by scheduling a manager's briefing several weeks before the program begins.

Just as each workshop begins with reports on the prior sessions' action plans and the progress made to date in implementing them, so should each workshop end with a summary of the various actions that different participants plan to take as a result of attending the workshop. This gives you feedback on the value (utility) of the concepts and techniques just taught. It also serves to help reluctant or uncreative participants whose eyes are opened as they listen to their colleagues share ideas on how they plan to apply their new learning back on the job.

Similarly, we recommend that the final session of your training program be devoted to a summary of the results of the action plans that have been implemented to date. This recap meeting might be scheduled a month or so after the last workshop session. Guidelines for conducting such a meeting are contained in Chapter 20.

ACTION PLAN

SUBJECT	State the specific area(s) or topics you have picked for improvement.

OBJECTIVE	What do you want to accomplish? What is your purpose, or broad objective?

GOALS	How will you know what you've accomplished? Your specific targets or yardsticks by which you will measure improvement.

PROBLEMS	SOLUTIONS
What barriers, resistance, interruptions, obstacles (anticipated and unforeseen) might you encounter as you implement your action plan? Number them.	How do you plan to avoid or to deal with the problems that you've just enumerated? Number to correspond with your list at the left.

RESOURCES

What people will you need to implement this plan? Time required? (Did you include your own time?) What other resources—equipment, materials, outside assistance?

ACTIVITIES	List in sequence the steps required to bring about the desired change. Indicate the time period for each in the column to the right, using actual calendar dates and estimates of the number of hours required for each activity listed.	**TIME**

COSTS

List the costs of implementing your action plan, including both initial capital investments (if any) and any changes in operating costs.

BENEFITS

Itemize the dollar benefits and estimate the value of any intangible benefits.

COMMITMENT

In signing below, we agree to make the commitment of time and money needed to carry out this action plan as outlined. We further agree to meet at the time(s) noted below to review progress and modify the schedule of activities described on page 3 as may be needed to achieve our goals and thereby meet our objectives.

Signatures: Date/Time for Progress Review(s)

_____   _____

_____   _____

Today's date: _____   _____

Individual Development Plan

Name: _____   Dept./Unit/Location: _____

Date of entry	Area targeted for improvement (competencies and styles)	Goal to be met or problem to be corrected (reason for selecting)	Proficiency		Actions to be taken (including persons who will help)	Time period	Date for evaluating results
			Actual %	Desired %			

CHAPTER 19

MEASURING TRAINING'S ROI

Upon completing this chapter you should be able to

◆ list courses on which you would not calculate return-on-investment (ROI)

◆ state at least five reasons why trainers avoid Level 4 evaluations

◆ list at least five reasons for calculating costs and benefits of training

◆ describe four ways to estimate or measure ROI on training

◆ explain: "Most cost-benefit analyses are comparative studies."

"Training doesn't cost—it pays! HRD is an investment, not an expense."

Rare is the trainer who doesn't believe this. Unfortunately, many of these same trainers do not believe that a return on the training investment can be calculated—or even should be. I'm reminded of the debate that went on some 30 years ago when programmed instruction (self-study) was just emerging. What kinds of courses can and can't be programmed? That was the burning question. B.F. Skinner at Harvard provided a simple answer: "You tell me what behavior you expect after the course, in observable, measurable terms, and I'll program it." Like Skinner, we can calculate the ROI on any course that has measurable, behavioral outcomes; for behaviors have values that can be either calculated or estimated.

Should all training programs be required to show an ROI? Not at all. However, courses of three days or more that are offered many times to reach a large number of trainees (100 or more) represent a significant expense. The professional trainer should justify this expense by calculating the return on this investment.

We're talking about Level 4 (results) on Donald Kirkpatrick's evaluation model, and it's the most difficult one to measure. Level 1 (reaction) and Level 2 (learning) can be measured with relative ease in class, using paper-and-pencil instruments and simulations. Level 3 (behavior at work) is more difficult, since it means measuring performance on the job where many variables are affecting the performance of our graduates. Level 4 is usually shown as an ROI—the value in dollars of the benefits of training over and above the cost of the training.

And there's the rub. Many factors make this level of measurement the most difficult by far. Here are some of the more common difficulties that are cited as reasons for not doing a Level 4 evaluation:

◆ The costs of training are known and expressed in dollars, but the benefits are often soft, subjective, and difficult to quantify and convert to dollars.

◆ We have enough trouble getting managers to send people to training without imposing additional requirements to collect data to document the impact.

◆ Costs are known up front, before training, but benefits may accrue slowly over time. At what point after training do you attempt to measure impact?

◆ As trainers, we lack the time and the needed accounting skills to do a cost-benefit analysis. Besides, our requests for data are disruptive of productivity.

◆ We will probably continue to run most of our training programs that are popular even if costs exceed benefits. So why bother? We're not a profit center.

◆ The outcomes could be damaging to the HRD staff and to budget support from top management. We may be better off in not knowing.

◆ People at work perform the way they do for many reasons, only one of which relates to training. How can we take credit or blame for their performance?

◆ The very act of collecting data on the dollar value of performance will tend to bias the information we get, making it hard for us to present a true picture.

If you've been looking for some reasons for not evaluating the ROI of your training efforts, read no further. This list should enable you to persuade the most insistent believer that any attempt to prove that training pays for itself is sheer folly! Let sleeping dogs lie—what we don't know can't hurt us. Right?

Wrong! Lest we be accused of favoritism, let's give equal time to a list of reasons why we should take the time and effort to calculate the costs and the benefits of our major training programs. Here are some supporting reasons:

◆ HRD budgets can be justified and even expanded when training can contribute to profit and is not seen as an act of faith or a cost of doing business.

◆ Course objectives and content will become more lean, relevant, and behavioral with focus on dollar results rather than on the acquisition of information.

- ◆ Better commitment of trainees and their managers, who become responsible for follow-up and ROI, and not just for filling seats.

- ◆ Action plans, individual development plans, and manager's briefings will be taken seriously, thus strengthening the trainee-manager partnership.

- ◆ Better performance by HRD staff in containing costs and maximizing benefits. They become performance managers and not just instructors.

- ◆ HRD staff has solid data on where training is effective and where it is weak, so that courses can be revised and fine-tuned to produce the best returns.

- ◆ The curriculum of courses offered can be determined on a financial basis and not just on popularity or the rank of the manager requesting it.

- ◆ Course enrollments will be serious, with trainees aware of the expectations that follow graduation. We'll get the right faces in the right places at the right times.

- ◆ By calculating ROI on the courses where it is possible, we are more apt to be trusted on the ones we can't evaluate at Level 4.

Now that we've examined the pros and cons of calculating the ROI of a training program, let's look at four ways of doing so. The nature of the training and the course objectives will determine which method is most appropriate.

Four Ways to Measure ROI on Training

When hard data exists. Performance data is routinely collected on many jobs for which we provide training. Examples include driver safety (dollar value of reduced accidents, lower insurance); machine maintenance (fewer repairs, less downtime); sales training (increased volume, fewer returns); and bank tellers (fewer overages and shortages, more services and customers handled per hour).

Many technical training programs have data on existing performance before the course was launched. By comparing the costs of inadequate performance prior to training with the reduced costs of better performance after training, we can see the ROI. Even courses that teach soft skills can have a hard data side to performance. Examples include writing skills (time saved via shorter letters, understood without subsequent clarification); meeting leadership (shorter meetings, better follow-up); EEO and diversity (fewer grievances and lawsuits). Notice that our examples focus on the quantitative aspects of performance—things that can be counted in minutes, dollars saved or gained. To be sure, these courses also have qualitative aspects of performance. But these are more difficult to quantify (courteous driving, more professional selling, clearer writing, more participative meeting leadership). Hard data probably doesn't exist to evaluate these qualities, so we have no way of comparing pretraining and posttraining performance.

Conclusion: If we want to take credit for the impact of training on workplace performance, we must establish a bench level of what the performance was before we launched the training program.

Estimates by trainees and their managers. This method is the easiest way to estimate ROI, but also the most subjective. Several months after completing each cycle of a training program, send a memo to each graduate and manager (sponsor). State the actual cost to the organization of the trainee's participation in the course. Ask the two to get together, discuss the actual improved performance that has taken place since the course, agree on a dollar value of this improvement, and project the total value of this improvement over the coming year (or whatever period is appropriate to the application of the concepts and skills that were learned). The two then send this projected dollar value in, along with a one- to two-paragraph explanation of how the estimate was determined. By comparing the costs of those who responded with their dollar estimates of value added to workplace performance, we can arrive at a crude estimate of the cost-benefit ratio.

In situations where bench levels were not established before the course was launched, this method of estimating ROI has appeal. What it lacks in accuracy it makes up for in getting trainees and their managers to recognize that the responsibility for making training effective is primarily theirs and not the trainer's.

Action plans; managers' briefing. During the course of a training program, each participant prepares an action plan that spells out how the concepts and skills being learned will be applied back at work. If the course involves the teaching of the entire job to a new employee, then the action plan will resemble a job description. If the course is for present employees (supervisors, team leaders, project managers), then the action plan spells out those actions the participant will take back to the job, which will differ from other participants whose needs are different.

After the training program, participants share their action plans with their managers and anyone else who is a stakeholder in their ongoing growth and development. This helps to build the participants' managers into their development—as coaches, mentors, and overseers of the implementation of the action plan. (A pretraining meeting with the participants' managers is important to cover objectives of the course, how the action plans work, and their role in helping their enrollees on the posttraining follow-through.)

Several months after the training, participants and their managers come together for a two- to three-hour meeting at which each participant reports on the actions taken as a result of implementing the action plan, along with the cost of doing so and the value of the benefits. Managers work with their participants prior to this meeting to arrive at the dollar value of the costs and the benefits. By tallying the numbers reported by the participants and adding the cost of the course, the ROI is obtained.

Cost-benefit analysis via accounting. This method is the most demanding way to calculate ROI, but also the most accurate. **Costs** can be listed under seven categories, as noted below:

◆ Course development (time) or purchase (price, license fees)

◆ Course materials: per participant (expendables) and instructor (durables)

◆ Equipment and hardware: projectors, computers, video ("fair share" use)

◆ Facilities: rental of conference center or fair share use of classroom overhead

◆ Travel, lodging, meals, breaks, shipping of materials

◆ Salary: of instructor and support staff (prorated), consultant's fees

◆ Lost productivity or cost of temporary replacements of participants.

These costs are of three types: one-time (needs analysis and design), cost per offering (facility rental, instructor's salary), and cost per participant (meals, notebooks, coffee breaks). Costs must therefore be calculated over the life of the training program.

Benefits fall into four major categories as shown below:

◆ Time savings (less time to reach proficiency, less supervision needed)

◆ Better quantity (faster work rate, less downtime, not having to wait for help)

◆ Better quality (fewer rejects, lost sales, reduced accidents, lower legal costs)

◆ Personnel data (less absenteeism, fewer medical claims, reduced grievances)

Benefits accrue long after training, and can be projected over the life of the trainees in the job for which they were trained (typically one to five years). While costs can be calculated by HRD managers, the benefits should be calculated by the trainees and their managers after they have had enough experience in the workplace to collect enough data to project the benefits over the payback period. A comparison of the total costs to the total benefits yields our ROI. A two-page cost-benefit worksheet is printed in chapter 22.

Observations on Conducting a Cost-Benefit Analysis

Some courses should be offered without expectation of measurable ROI (orientation of new employees, retirement planning). Since the benefits of conducting such programs are difficult if not impossible to measure, and since organizations offer them without expectation of any tangible ROI, it is foolish to attempt a cost-benefit analysis.

Training programs for employees whose jobs have well-defined and quantified expectations (standards, goals, quotas) are the most appropriate ones for measuring return on the training investment since performance measurement systems already exist.

In contrast, training for supervisors, managers, technical experts, project coordinators, and others for whom performance measurement systems do not exist are much more difficult to evaluate via Level 4 (cost-benefit analysis). The responsibility rests with each trainee to generate pretraining data and posttraining data on performance, and to assign dollar values to these two sets of data.

Most cost-benefit analyses are comparative studies that show how the performance levels obtained by installing a new training program compare with the performance levels obtained by no training (safety, drugs, stress reduction) or by some alternative form of training (on-the-job training vs. classroom, individualized vs. group, centralized vs. regional). As above, pretraining data on performance prior to installation of the new program may not have been collected. This must be done prior to carrying out a cost-benefit analysis.

When training is conducted to accompany the installation of new equipment (procedures, products, policies, technology) and no prior training of a similar nature existed, a cost-benefit analysis is inappropriate for two reasons. First, there are no prior performance measures with which to compare the results of the new training. And second, the impact of installing the new changes makes it impossible to separate performance attributable to training from performance attributable to innovation. (Examples include moving from manual to PC operations and learning to use e-mail).

The costs of training are known up front and should be calculated by HRD managers and others whose budget is funding the program. The major unknown is based on the shelf life of the course—how many times (cycles) it will be run before it is no longer needed (all eligible trainees have received it or changes in technology have rendered it obsolete). Costs should be calculated over the shelf life of the program.

Similarly, the benefits of training should extend well beyond the final offering (cycle) of the program. Different behaviors that were shaped by training have a different life cycle. The payback period on skills that are practiced regularly (for example, time management) might be projected over the employment life of the trainee, whereas skills that are called on less frequently (selection interviewing in a downsized economy) may have a much shorter payback period.

Although the costs of training are best calculated by HRD managers, the benefits should be identified, quantified, and converted to dollar values by management (the trainees' supervisors, department heads). There are two reasons for this. First, they are in the best position to observe changes in performance attributable to training; and second, their data is more objective and less suspect than if HRD specialists attempted to collect it.

Examples of Applications of Cost-Benefit Analysis

1. A rapidly growing fast-food chain had a three-week apprentice training program that prepared employees for promotion to assistant manager. The corporate HRD manager thought training time could be reduced to one week with a formal training program at headquarters. The one-week formal program required travel and hotel costs not associated with the three-week local apprentice training program. However, the company's ability to place assistant managers in outlets two weeks earlier resulted in savings that more than offset the cost of developing the program and bringing the trainees to a central location. It also ensured uniform quality of instruction, which was lacking in the decentralized apprentice training that had taken place in each outlet.

2. A major corporation had relied on two professors from the state university to come in and conduct their supervisory training program, using their own handouts, visuals, and hands-on exercises. Ninety-three supervisors went through the five-day program in classes of 15 to 16 participants each. Three years later when the company offered supervisory training again, they purchased a packaged course with videos, workbooks, and instructor guidelines for their own internal instructors. Although the package cost $27,000, they ended up saving $16,000 (the professors had charged $36,000 for labor and $7,000 for materials). Moreover, postworkshop evaluations showed that transfer of training from workshop to workplace had improved significantly.

3. A government agency ran a three-day workshop on project management, in six offerings for 20 participants each. During the year following each workshop, the trainers surveyed the graduates to see how their posttraining performance on projects compared with their pretraining behavior (as assessed during the needs analysis prior to training). Factors evaluated included: (a) degree of projects completed on time and within budget; (b) level of client satisfaction; and (c) estimate of time and money saved as a result of improved project management. The agency concluded that a $95,000 training investment had saved an estimated $670,000. This figure did not include one reported savings of $2 million projected over a five-year period and agreed to by the graduate and her manager.

4. An automotive manufacturer installed a management development program as part of the company's Total Quality Management/empowerment efforts and ran 220 managers at an assembly plant through the program. The average length was six days. After the first day of

assessment, each manager attended only those workshops that dealt with the competencies and skills that received lower scores. Six months after the training, participants were again assessed. Benefits were evaluated on three factors: (a) the degree to which each manager's individual development plan had been implemented; (b) the change in productivity of the manager's work group; and (c) the improvement in scores (percentiles against nationwide norms) by each manager on the two assessments. All three measures showed the benefits far outweighed the costs.

CHAPTER 20

USING MANAGEMENT BRIEFINGS

Upon completing this chapter you should be able to

◆ state at least four benefits of posttraining recap meetings

◆ explain how ROI can be calculated at the recap meeting

◆ indicate the ideal length of time between training and recap meeting

◆ list the key items to be addressed in each trainee's report

◆ describe cases where three to four trainees might work on one action plan.

In chapter 18 we discussed the managers' briefing that is held several weeks before a new course is launched. The purpose is to win support of the participants' managers to the course objectives and to their role in reviewing the action plans and in attending a second manager's briefing after the course (the recap meeting) at which each participant will report briefly (average: five minutes) on the results obtained back on the job. This chapter describes that second meeting.

The purpose and date for the recap meeting should be given to the participants' managers at the precourse managers' briefing. This should serve to reinforce the three-way partnership between instructor, participants, and their managers. Effective training requires the commitment and active participation of all three if the course is to be fully effective. Here are some of the benefits of making the recap meeting part of the course design:

◆ Both parties will take the action plans and individual development plans more seriously and be committed to implementing them.

◆ No supervisor or manager wants to be embarrassed in front of peers by ineffective reports from members of their staff or work group.

◆ Similarly, no participant wants to come to the recap meeting with nothing to report (no success stories following the course).

◆ The cumulative effect of hearing positive reports helps to foster renewed commitment to apply at work what was learned in class.

◆ The instructor can get an excellent evaluation of the course's impact at Level 3 (behavior) and Level 4 (results).

◆ The individual reports by participants give managers a good overview of the leadership potential of the graduates.

The recap meeting should be a day of celebration. Make this day your graduation with end-of-course certificates and a wine-and-cheese reception (or perhaps a meal for supervisory training or management development programs). Participants should be told in advance to come to the recap meeting with estimates of the costs in implementing their plan and the benefits, expressed in dollar values. As they give their reports, the instructor can tally the total costs and benefits, and report these figures to the group: "Many of you noticed that I was adding up your costs and your benefits as you gave your reports. And I'm pleased to announce that the benefits come to $118,000, while the costs totaled about $6,000. That's a 20-to-1 return on the investment of your time. Congratulations!"

If participants are not accustomed to making brief presentations, you can add structure to the exercise and make their jobs easier by sending out a one-page questionnaire for them to complete and use as their report outline. After the recap meeting, you can collect these for use in putting together a success story for senior management, and possibly for publication in the employee newspaper or a trade journal (of the training field or of the industry group to which your company belongs).

Here are examples of some of the questions to be included in your one-page questionnaire that will help participants prepare for their presentations:

1. What areas (needs, problems, opportunities, responsibilities) did you work on to improve performance following the training program?

2. How did you go about this? What actions did you take?

3. What tangible, measurable results did you see to show whether or not your efforts were paying off?

4. What did it cost in time and money? (Use actual estimates of hours and dollars.)

5. What savings or benefits have you seen to date as a result of the actions you have taken?

As participants give their reports, they should be reminded that the answers to questions 4 and 5 are being given at one point of time, whereas the costs and benefits might be projected over a payback period of months and perhaps years. The longer the payback period, the greater the potential return on the initial training investment. (Chapter 21 gives an example of how the payback period on a training program was estimated.)

In courses where participants have attended a different lesson (topic, session) for each day or half-day of class, tell them to select one or two of the topics for their report rather than trying to cover everything. Similarly, although the four-page action plan has 10 sections to the form, participants should simplify their presentations and go with the five questions just outlined.

An invitation memo to the recap meeting should go out to participants and their managers several weeks before the event. Arrange for a senior manager to send out the invitations and to be present at the meeting to congratulate the graduates and their managers. Plan the length of your recap meeting in advance, and indicate this in the invitation memo. Such meetings normally last 90-120 minutes.

If your class size is 20 or fewer, the graduates can make their action plan reports to the managers as a full group. With larger numbers, the reports can become repetitive and take too long. The solution is to have individual tables seating four to eight participants and their managers (usually three to five, since many managers send more than one participant to the training program). With this arrangement, reports can be made simultaneously at each table. With classes in which participants from the same departments or work areas are learning how to implement new programs (for example, Total Quality Management, Employee Involvement), you may find it appropriate to encourage participants at the start of the training to work together on their action plan and to be prepared to present it at the recap meeting as a team effort.

The amount of time allowed to pass between the last training session and the recap meeting depends on the time required to implement the action plans and the length of the payback period needed to realize a return on the training investment. On courses that teach skills that are immediately applicable or procedures that have just been changed, an interim of three to four weeks might be appropriate. Twice this long would apply to courses for supervisors and managers.

A key to the success of your recap meeting is the informality of the climate. This can be improved by having whatever refreshments you plan to serve available as people arrive. Background music from a cassette player can also help to establish a relaxed atmosphere.

CHAPTER 21

MEASURING ROI VIA ACTION PLANS

Upon reading this case study you should be able to

◆ describe at least three organizational needs for supervisory training

◆ indicate the advantage of having class every other week

◆ explain why senior management saw the 15-to-1 ROI as conservative

◆ list at least four factors behind the successful ROI in San Antonio.

In the prior chapter we examined some of the benefits of planning a recap meeting a month or so after your course is over so that your graduates can report to their managers and fellow participants on the results of applying at work what they learned in class (their success in implementing the action plans). This chapter contains a case study that describes the role that action plans and the recap meeting played in enabling The Coca-Cola Bottling Company of San Antonio to realize a return on investment of 15 to 1. Their 64 supervisors who went through the training program managed to generate or save $526,000 over and above the $34,000 cost of running the program. This case study began about a year before the recap meeting. Here's the story.

As part of a five-day workshop for presidents and general managers of its franchised bottlers, The Coca-Cola Company surveyed participants to determine the developmental needs of their employees. In every location that the workshop was conducted throughout the United States, results were identical: The need for supervisory training led the list. Several reasons were cited. (1) No such program for bottlers existed. (2) Some bottlers had hired local consultants or professors to run courses for their supervisors with little or no impact on performance. (3) Supervisors are the primary source of training for all other employees. (4) The legal implications and cost of poor supervisory practices were rising at a rapid rate. (5) The era of father-to-son-to-grandson management of bottling plants was drawing to a close. Future managers would come from the ranks and not from the family that owned the franchise.

In response to this need, The Coca-Cola Company selected a consultant who would develop a series of half-day workshops to be run by bottlers. Since most of the franchised bottlers do not have a professional trainer on staff, the workshops would be designed to be taught by members of senior management: department heads and officers. Detailed instructor guidelines and train-the-trainer workshops would be needed to make the program as user-friendly as possible. The consultant surveyed the bottlers of Coca-Cola, using a questionnaire to rank a list of 20 supervisory needs as high, moderate, or low. This data was analyzed and the top eight topics were selected for development. The Coca-Cola Bottling Company of San Antonio was selected as the first pilot for the training.

Needs of the Organization

Although the needs analysis conducted via questionnaires was useful in identifying the developmental needs of bottling plant supervisors, the San Antonio bottler also had a number of organizational needs that they hoped training could address. With a market of more than a million customers, the company had been growing rapidly and had formed several new divisions (food service, canteen vending, lunch trucks, and metered bar service). With this new growth came many newly appointed supervisors who were more comfortable handling their old job than supervising people. This meant that senior managers were handling problems that should have been resolved at the supervisory level.

Another organizational need sprang from major changes in the way the products reached market. In earlier times, the bottlers of Coca-Cola relied on route salesmen to take orders, deliver product, and stack the shelves in larger outlets. The proliferation of many new products and package sizes, however, had led to a reorganization of the means of distribution. Sales were now made by telephone ("tel-sell" representatives) and by face-to-face calls (customer service representatives). Deliveries were made by three types of truck, depending on outlet size. And the stacking and displaying of product in the outlets were handled by a newly created position: merchandisers. This reorganization created new supervisory positions and led to the need for training.

Newly appointed supervisors often show stronger allegiance to their team of employees than to management, whose ranks they have recently joined. This factor weighed heavily on the minds of senior management. The company had managed to resist past efforts by the union to organize the employees. The prior vote had been very close, however, and management feared that the uncertainty surrounding the reorganization and the supervision that employees were receiving could give the union the edge they needed to win the next election, about a half-year away.

The Course Is Launched

Twelve members of senior management served as instructors. They included the executive vice president and his division heads and officers. These 12 were participants in the first cycle of the course, taught by the consultant. Their focus was on content and process: what to teach and how (instructional methods, media, techniques). The group agreed to use team teaching, with two managers assigned to each of the eight modules of the course. (Some of the managers were responsible for more than one module.) These modules were as follows:

◆ Your Role as Supervisor

◆ Defining the Job and Performance Criteria

◆ Setting Goals and Standards

◆ Training and Developing the Team

◆ Conducting Performance Reviews

◆ Motivating and Managing Others

◆ Managing Your Time Effectively

◆ Personnel Policies and Procedures

With 64 supervisors to be trained, the bottler divided them into four groups of 16 participants each: the Tuesday group, Wednesday group, and so on. Participants attended class one week and met with their managers individually the following week to agree on how they would implement the actions they planned to take as a result of attending the workshop. Thus, every other week brought a different module, and the entire program took 16 weeks to administer.

Slides and audiotape script provided the concepts and informational input for each workshop, followed by hands-on learning exercises: role plays, case method, games, simulations, script analysis, and action plans. The selection of slides enabled each bottler to replace scenes with locally shot slides, thereby customizing and personalizing the instruction. Another benefit of the slides was that they were used interactively. After each key learning point (every six to eight slides), a "discussion slide" posed two to three questions. By spending three or four minutes discussing these questions, the instructors enabled the participants to apply new concepts and skills to their own jobs and employees.

Detailed instructor guidelines made it possible for the bottler's own senior managers to deliver the workshops with confidence and competence. The relevance and credibility of each module was seen as very high by participants who knew that it was important enough for the "top brass" to be teaching it and drawing on their own experience to illustrate the learning points.

Action Plans: Key to High Transfer

Transfer of training refers to the degree to which participants apply in the workplace what they acquired in the workshop. Most trainers estimate the degree of transfer for soft skills courses such as supervisory training at a relatively low level: 20 to 40% according to a survey of more than 1,000 training managers. In short, they see little ROI for such courses.

To overcome the tendency of supervisors to view training as a spectator sport (watching an instructor perform), the consultant built the process of action planning into each module of the training. Action plans can be viewed as a means of putting management by objectives into operation among first-level supervisors whose typical day is activity oriented and reactive rather than goal oriented and proactive. It's a way of getting supervisors to manage and to launch their own program of continuous improvement.

Calculating the ROI

The Coca-Cola Bottling Company of San Antonio did not make a conscious decision to calculate ROI following the training program. However, management's decision to bring the 64 supervisors together three months after the course for a final executive briefing and graduation dinner enabled them to collect data on the program's impact. Each of the four groups of 16 supervisors met for two hours, and each participant took five to 10 minutes to report on the results they had achieved by applying the concepts and skills learned in class and translated into on-the-job behavior on their action plans (increased sales, reduced waste, shorter collection times, better route planning, less absenteeism). The audience for these briefings consisted of the senior managers who had taught the program and helped their subordinate supervisors to follow through on their action plans. Each supervisor and his manager calculated the cost of implementing each action plan (mostly time rather than additional expense). They also converted the benefits and payoff into estimates of dollar value (savings or additional revenues). In short, each supervisor's report on their follow-up on eight action plans was actually a mini cost-benefit analysis of the impact of the course.

Following the four briefing sessions of two hours each, the company hosted a graduation dinner during which the HRD manager and consultant tallied the total of the costs and benefits reported. Results: The company had realized an ROI of $526,000 over and above the $34,000 cost of running the training program. In short, the benefits exceeded the cost by more than 15 to 1. Senior management considered this figure conservative since many supervisors did not attach dollar values to the benefits realized by implementing their action plans. Moreover, no value was assigned to the results of the election in which the union's attempt to organize the bottler was defeated by a significant margin. Management attributed this victory to a greatly improved climate in the workplace, and saw this benefit alone as having a value over time in the millions of dollars.

Perhaps the most conservative aspect of the 15-to-1 ratio is the fact that most supervisors were reporting their benefits for a three-month period (the time lapsed since the end of the course). Most of the savings and increased revenues are ongoing, however, and could be projected to continue for at least several years into the future. A key lesson here is that training costs occur at one point in time whereas many training benefits are ongoing and should be projected well beyond the life of the course. Although the figures reported are conservative, they are dramatic and impressive. Everyone at the graduation banquet felt the heady exhilaration of their achievements.

Factors Contributing to ROI

Why was this training so successful as installed in San Antonio? Let's begin by dispelling a myth. Supervisory training is not a soft skills course unless it is taught that way. There are hundreds of very specific behaviors that apply to anyone who supervises. These can be pinpointed, described, illustrated, and practiced in class, then shared with one's manager after class so that both parties become accountable for applying these behaviors on the job. Moreover, supervisory training has the potential for a much greater impact on the organization than does skills training for nonsupervisory personnel. A supervisor of 10 persons has a multiplier effect of 10. By improving the performance of most or all of these 10 employees, the supervisor can generate a much greater return on the training investment.

A number of factors contributed to the successful ROI obtained in San Antonio. None of these factors taken alone would have had a significant impact. Taken cumulatively, however, their effect is powerful. Here are the major ones:

Top management as instructors. It is the responsibility of managers to develop their staff. When they serve as instructors, the message takes on more credibility, immediacy, and relevance. They are also in an excellent position to follow up on the action plans for their own "direct report" supervisors, having taught the modules. The training of supervisors is too important to be left to trainers, who can do it in partnership with management (but who shouldn't be left to do it for management). Some things can't be delegated. The raising of your children is one. The development of your supervisors is another.

Participative course design. Supervisors were active throughout each workshop. New concepts and skills were presented deductively (discovery method) rather than inductively (lecture method). Links in the instructional chain were small and strong (stimulus-response-feedback links ran an average of six to eight minutes each). Participants worked in subgroups of three or four persons each, thereby giving maximum hands-on learning opportunity to every participant.

Action plans. These four-page planning sheets got supervisors to commit their time and resources to transferring new concepts and skills from workshop to workplace. They also served to forge a partnership between each participant and his or her manager so that new behavior is recognized and reinforced (maintained) back on the job.

Executive briefing. By scheduling graduation day several months after a course is over, participants have time to follow through on their action plans and begin to show results. Since their managers don't want to be embarrassed by having participants with nothing to report (that is, no ROI), there's a strong incentive for managers to follow through with their supervisors' action plans.

Calculation of costs and benefits. Traditionally, management has been responsible for controlling costs and maximizing benefits. Companies preach that "it's everybody's job" but have never had supervisors and workers calculate the dollar value of their efforts and their results. By getting participants to go through this process for each module of the course, they develop the skills and the habit of thinking like a manager.

Instruction in goal setting. Following the introductory module (Your Role as Supervisor), the next two modules taught the dos and don'ts of setting goals and standards. Without this, supervisors and managers tend to describe wishes or activities when asked for goals. The quality of their action plan goals is much better when they know the difference and can evaluate the measurability of their goals and standards.

Taking time to do it right. The consultant took a year to create the training program, and the bottler took over eight months to implement it (one month to prepare senior management, four months to run the program, three months before graduation day). Many supervisory training programs are run as a five-day course, with little or no opportunity to develop action plans and discuss them with managers. By scheduling one workshop every two weeks and allowing three months after the course for germination, the harvest (yield) is much greater.

This case study illustrates how ROI can be calculated for supervisory training programs. Each participant and his or her manager is given the responsibility for follow-through on action plans that spell out (a) how the concepts and skills taught in class will be applied on the job; and (b) how the costs and benefits of this implementation will be evaluated (measured and converted to dollar value). The cumulative result of all participants' implementation of their action plans generated during the course thus becomes a cost-benefit analysis that measures the impact of training and the ROI.

CHAPTER 22

MEASURING ROI VIA COST-BENEFIT ANALYSIS

Upon completing this chapter you should be able to

◆ list seven categories of cost and four categories of benefits

◆ give several examples of fixed and of variable costs of training

◆ describe how the length of a payback period might be determined

◆ indicate which categories of costs and benefits apply to your course(s)

◆ carry out a cost-benefit analysis.

Recall the four levels at which a training program can be evaluated (the Kirkpatrick model in chapter 1): 1. Reaction (Did the participants like it?); 2. Learning (Did they learn what was taught?); 3. Behavior (Did they use it back at work?); and 4. Results (Did it produce a return on the investment?)

The first two can be measured in class, or before a course is over. The last two must be measured in the workplace, after a course is over and some time has passed so that we can measure long-term impact and not merely immediate application. Of the four levels listed above, the last one is by far the most difficult to evaluate. Data collection is time consuming and sometimes disruptive of productive work. Moreover, the cause-and-effect relationship between a training program and the subsequent performance of its graduates back on the job is never as clean and direct as we would like. Nevertheless, it is often desirable that trainers carry out a cost-benefit analysis and attempt to measure the impact of training in dollars saved or earned as a result of training and the major benefits.

When conducting a cost-benefit analysis, we consider seven categories of **costs:** course development, instructional (materials, equipment), facilities, off-site expenses, salary, and lost productivity. Some organizations count the salary paid to participants during the time they are in class as a cost of training. Others regard training as part of their job—just as productive as any other activity, and therefore not a cost to be charged (debited) to training.

Similarly, we consider four categories of **benefits:** time savings (reaching proficiency sooner), better productivity, improved quality of work, and better personnel performance. The first three can be measured individually on each graduate, while the last one is concerned with organizational statistics (absenteeism, tardiness, health or accident costs, jobs eliminated).

Keep these categories in mind as you read the case study that follows. In it you will find the numbers and information needed to complete the calculations to carry out a cost-benefit analysis on the sample form provided.

Case Study: Running Effective Meetings Workshop at Southwest Industries

Southwest Industries was no different from other organizations their size (about 900 employees) when it came to time spent in meetings. Their managers felt that time was wasted, key players were often absent, and agendas were not followed (or, in some cases, even established). Their training manager decided to do something about it. Using a questionnaire and group interviews with managers in each department, she came up with the design for a half-day workshop to meet the following objectives:

1. **Reduced length of meetings.** Managers estimated the average meeting to run about 75 minutes and hoped this could be reduced to under one hour.

2. **Reduced frequency of meetings.** Managers attended an average of 8.6 meetings per week and hoped to reduce this to 5.0 or fewer.

3. **Better follow-up and execution.** Many decisions reached at meetings didn't get acted on until the next meeting or a reminder.

4. **Appropriate participants attend.** No time is wasted because key people were absent and unnecessary people were present.

5. **Better decisions and stronger commitment.** By teaching the use of a decision matrix, decisions should be more effective.

The training manager sent these objectives and a cover memo to the company's 95 managers and supervisors, who approved them and added two more, shown on the next page. They also suggested that a workshop on how to run meetings shouldn't be restricted to managers, since about 250 employees were members of work teams of eight to 10 persons each. These teams typically held one-hour meetings once a week to address problems and improve quality. Here are the two additional training objectives:

6. **Effective problem solving.** By teaching the process and applying it to typical work-related problems.

7. **Timely minutes for follow-up.** Minutes are often distributed too late to be effective and unclear as to actions to be taken.

During the development of the workshop's methods and materials, the training manager realized that a half-day workshop would not have the desired impact. For example, the ability to prepare results-oriented and measurable objectives for a meeting is important to its success. This meant preparing an exercise in which participants evaluate and rewrite a dozen typical meeting objectives and designing two forms that required time for participants to get hands-on practice in using them (a meeting announcement form and a recap form). Consequently, Running Effective Meetings ended up as a one-day workshop (6.5 hours). Other than one learning exercise that was different for the 95 managers and supervisors and for the 250 team members, the workshop was the same for both groups.

Costs of the Workshop

The workshop was offered 15 times, with an average enrollment of 21 participants—off site to get participants away from the interruptions at the plant. A nearby motel charged $20 per person to cover coffee break, lunch buffet, and afternoon soda and snack. The room itself cost $100 per day.

Other costs of the course were minimal. The biggest expense was the training manager's time in preparing the objectives and getting feedback (one day), preparing course material (five days), and running the program (15 days). The 22 pages of handouts took three days for the administrative assistant to type and lay out (desktop publishing). Thereafter, the cost of reproducing, collating, and inserting handouts in folders came to about $2 per participant. The set of 12 colored overhead transparencies cost about $150 to make.

The training manager felt that it would not be appropriate to consider the salaries of participants (during their day at the workshop) to be a cost of training, and her manager agreed. Similarly, the cost of any productivity lost due to attendance at the workshop was not seen as a cost of training. However, the administrative assistant did spend a total of two hours on each of the 15 workshops in scheduling participants and sending out the invitations.

Benefits of the Workshop

The workshop handouts included a log that participants were asked to make entries on following each meeting they attended during the three months after going through the workshop. An analysis of the entries on the 264 logs that were returned indicated the following data (listed in the same sequence as the seven objectives identified earlier):

1. The average length of a management meeting was 55 minutes, a savings of 20 minutes compared to the preworkshop average of 75 minutes. The length of work team meetings remained the same, about an hour.

2. Fewer meetings took place. During the three months following the workshop, managers attended an average of 5.6 meetings per week, down from the pretraining average of 8.6 meetings. (These figures came from the 65 managers who returned their logs. The change in frequency of meetings among members of work teams was not significant, since most teams continued to meet on a once-a-week basis.)

3. All respondents reported that the execution and follow-up had improved. No figures were asked for on this question on the log.

4. The responses indicated that three managers who had run their weekly departmental meetings with everyone present (a command performance) were now making participation voluntary on a need-to-know basis. Result: Over the 39 meetings held during the three months, 87 hours were freed up for people who had previously been required to attend.

5.-6. Respondents were asked to estimate the dollar value of better decision making and problem solving. Although participants indicated that they were using the processes taught in the workshop, only eight respondents indicated a dollar value. Their estimates ranged from $50 to $10,000. The training manager decided not to use this data in the cost-benefit analysis.

7. In the workshop, trainees were taught how to use a recap form during meetings to record any decisions, actions, or assignments. This made the writing and distributing of minutes unnecessary, yielding a savings of 45 minutes (average) per meeting on the part of the participant who served as recorder.

Given this information, the training manager was ready to calculate the dollar value of the time savings (on objectives 1, 2, 4, and 7) that the workshop had made possible. The improved performance reported in response to objectives 3, 5, and 6 was a qualitative estimate and hard to quantify, so it was not included in the calculations. Before doing the cost-benefit analysis, the training manager made the following assumptions and verified them by checking with the vice president of HRD and several other managers:

- The average annual salary of managers and supervisors at Southwest Industries is $52,000, which amounts to $1,000 per week, or $200 per day, or $25 per hour.

- The average annual salary of team members is $36,000, which amounts to $692 per week, or $138 per day, or $17 per hour.

- The cost of employee benefits at Southwest Industries (insurance, medical) is figured at 30% of salary. In other words, every employee is costing the company 130% of their gross salary.

◆ The meetings held by managers typically have about five persons in attendance (compared to the team meetings where nine members typically attend).

◆ The meetings included in the cost-benefit analysis are held at Southwest Industries and have no significant expense other than the salaries of participants. (Seminars, conventions, trade shows, and other meetings are excluded from the calculations.)

Now it's your turn. Put yourself in the training manager's shoes. Calculate the cost of the workshop and the benefits. You have all the information you need to estimate costs and benefits. You are working with benefits (savings) for the three months following the workshop, which can be entered on your worksheet as a savings "per participant per month" (last column). Then answer these questions:

◆ Did costs exceed benefits, or vice versa?

◆ By what amount? What ratio?

◆ Is a year too long, too short, or about right as the payback period?

◆ What was the cost per student-hour of this workshop?

◆ Is that high, low, or about average for company-run training? (Guess.)

This cost-benefit analysis is a standard (generic) form, so many of the categories of costs and benefits will not apply. Make entries only where applicable. When you've added up your costs and your benefits, read the solution to the case on the pages that follow and compare our calculations with yours.

COST-BENEFIT ANALYSIS

COSTS

	One-time costs	Cost per offering	Cost per participant

1. Course development (time) or selection (price, fees)

- needs analysis and research
- design and creation of blueprint
- writing and validating and revising
- producing (typesetting, illustrating, ready for reproducing)

2. Instructional materials

- per participant (expendables: notebooks, handouts, tests)
- per instructor (durables: videotape, film, PC software, overheads)

3. Equipment (hardware)

- projectors, VHS, computers, flipcharts, training aids

4. Facilities

- rental or allocated "fair share" usage of classrooms

5. Off-site expenses (if applicable)

- travel, hotel overnights, meals, breaks
- shipping of materials, rental of audiovisual equipment

6. Salary

- participants (no. hours instruction times average hourly rate)
- instructor, course administrator, program manager
- fees to consultants or outside instructors
- support staff (audiovisual, administrative)

7. Lost productivity (if applicable)

- production rate losses or material losses

- **A.** Total of all one-time up-front costs
- **B.** Total of all costs incurred each time course is offered
- **C.** This sum (B) times no. times course is run (___)
- **D.** Total of all costs incurred for each participant
- **E.** This sum (D) times no. participants (___) over life of course
- **F.** Total costs (sum of A, C, and E)

COST-BENEFIT ANALYSIS

BENEFITS

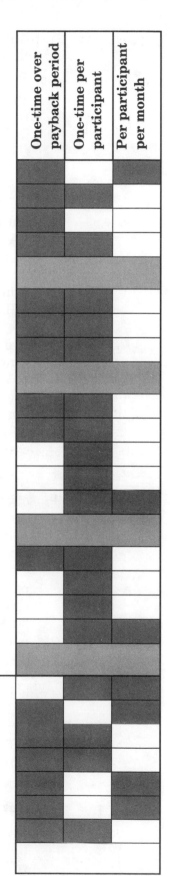

	One-time over payback period	One-time per participant	Per participant per month

1. Time savings

- shorter lead time to reach proficiency (hrs. saved times $)
- less time required to perform an operation (hrs. saved times $)
- less supervision needed (supervisory hrs. saved times supervisory $)
- better time management (hrs. freed up times $)

2. Better productivity (quantity)

- faster work rate ($ value of additional units, sales)
- time saved by not having to wait for help (hrs. saved times $)
- less downtime ($ value of reduced nonproductive time)

3. Improved quality of output

- fewer rejects (scrap, lost sales, returns—$ value)
- value added to output (bigger sales, smoother castings—$)
- reduced accidents ($ value of savings on claims, lost work)
- reduced legal costs (EEO, OSHA, workman's comp settlements—$)
- improved competitiveness (change in market share—$)

4. Better personnel performance (attributable to training)

- less absenteeism/tardiness (self or subordinates—$ saved)
- improved health ($ saved on medical and lost time)
- reduced grievances, claims, job actions ($ saved)
- same output with fewer employees ($ on jobs eliminated)

A. Total of all one-time benefits

B. Total of all benefits occurring once per participant

C. Total value of all improvements per participant per month

D. Length of payback period in months

E. Number of employees affected during this period (D)

F. Total of B times E

G. Total of C times D times E

H. Total benefits (sum of A, F, and G)

Costs of the Workshop (The Calculations at Southwest Industries)

The costs of researching, developing, and delivering 15 one-day workshops on Running Effective Meetings are relatively easy to calculate. The training manager spent one day on research and five days on the design and writing of the course material: a total of six days. We can assume that the training manager's salary is about $200 per day. The cost of benefits will add 30%. Thus, we enter $260 and $1,300 under "1. Course development" on the cost-benefit analysis form.

An administrative assistant took three days to type and lay out the materials. Assuming the salary to be about the same as a team member's, we have 3 × $138, or $414. Again, benefits will add 30% to this amount, so we enter $538 as the cost of production (typesetting and layout).

As for "2. Instructional materials," each participant received a presentation folder with handouts. This item cost about $2 to reproduce and collate, which we enter as the cost of participant materials.

There are two costs for the instructor: the $150 for the 12 overhead transparencies, which we enter under "One-time costs," and the $20 for lunch and breaks, which we enter under "Costs per offering."

Since the only equipment needed was an overhead projector, which the motel provided, there was no cost for "3. Equipment." (If the training manager had purchased a projector or if the course had accounted for a major usage of existing equipment, then it would be appropriate to add a cost for this course's "fair share" of the equipment.)

The next entry on the cost-benefit analysis form is for "4. Facilities." Since the room cost $100 per day, we can enter $100 under "Costs per offering."

As for "5. Off-site expenses," Southwest Industries was billed $20 per person to cover refreshments and lunch for each participant. Thus, we can enter $20 under "Costs per participant."

Under "6. Salary," it was decided not to include the salary of participants or "7. Lost productivity" as costs of training. However, the salary category that does apply is the instructor's time: $200 per day for salary and 30% for employee benefits, giving us $260, which we enter under "Costs per offering." Similarly, the administrative assistant spent two hours on each workshop in scheduling participants and sending out invitations. At $17 per hour, this comes to $34, which becomes $44 when we add 30% for benefits. So we enter $44 as a support staff cost under "Costs per offering."

If we add up the costs just itemized, and multiply by the number of offerings (15) and number of participants (315), they yield a total of $15,538. This is the sum of all costs in producing and running the one-day workshop 15 times.

Benefits of the Workshop

Now let's look at the benefits of training—the payback that Southwest Industries realized as a result of the workshop. This was calculated as the value of the time saved in addressing objectives 1, 2, 4, and 7.

On objective 1, the participants reported a savings of 20 minutes per meeting (average). This applied to meetings attended by managers, since the meetings of work teams did not change significantly. The company's 95 managers reported an average of 5.6 meetings per week, which converts ($\times$ 4.33) to 24.25 meetings per month. One-third of an hour is saved at each meeting, for a total of 8.08 hours saved per manager (.33 $\times$ 24.25). At $25 per hour, this savings amounts to $202, which we enter under "1. Time savings" as "better time management."

On objective 2, a major benefit was realized by reducing the number of meetings from 8.6 to 5.6, a savings of three meetings per week, or 13 meetings per month. Since the time managers spent at meetings had been averaging 75 minutes, or 1.25 hours, the monthly savings is 13 $\times$ 1.25, or 16.25 hours at $25 per hour, or $406. We can enter this under "2. Better productivity" as "less downtime" (value of reduced nonproductive time).

On objective 4, three respondents to the log and questionnaire reported a savings of 87 hours over the three months, for an average of 29 hours per month. Since the training manager didn't know whether managers or nonmanagers accounted for this savings, it was assumed they were nonmanagerial, so the salary figures for team members were applied: 29 hours $\times$ $17 gives us a savings of $493 per month. But this is not a "per participant" saving, so none of the three column headings on our benefits worksheet apply. The nearest heading is the first column's "one time" heading if we decide to make the length of the payback period one year (the 12 months following the workshop). So we multiply $493 by 12 to get a one-time saving of $5,916, which we can enter under "4. Better personnel performance" as "same output with fewer employees."

On objective 7, by having participants make their own notes (minutes) during meetings, there's a savings of 45 minutes (average) per meeting on the part of the recorder. To calculate this saving, we have to determine how many meetings were held during the month following the workshop. This number is different for managers and for work teams. Let's look at each.

Managers. Ninety-five managers attend 5.6 meetings per week, for a total of 532 attendees. However, the average number of managers at a meeting is five, so 532 divided by 5 comes to an average of 106 meetings per week $\times$ 45 minutes saved at each, for a savings of 79.5 hours per week, or 344 hours per month. This converts to 8.6 weeks (344 divided by 40) of a recorder's time saved each month. At $1,000 per week, managers freed from serving as recorders have saved $8,600 per month. This belongs under "1. Time savings" as "less time required to perform an operation." But none of the headings apply. So we divide by our 95 managers so that we can enter it in the last column as a "per participant" saving: $8,600 divided by 95 giving us $91.

Team members. We know that 250 employees are team members, and teams average nine members. Thus 250 divided by 9 gives us a total of 27.8 teams. They meet once a week, or 4.33 times per month, for a total of 27.8 $\times$ 4.33, or 120 meetings per month $\times$ 45 minutes (for recorder to prepare minutes). This is a savings of 90 hours, or 2.25 weeks, of recorders at $692 per week, for a total monthly savings of

$1,557. Now we can convert this to a "per participant" saving by dividing $1,557 by 250. We enter the result, $6, in the last column, sharing a box with the $91 figure for managers in our last entry.

Because our per participant savings are listed for two different populations (managers and team members), we will have to keep these figures separate when we multiply by the number of persons in each population.

Now we are ready to do the calculations at the bottom of the benefits columns so that the savings per month and per participant are extended over the total number of months (payback period) and the total number of employees affected. In this case, this is 95 and 250, a figure greater than the 315 participants, since the savings at meetings were realized by everyone who attended them and not just by the 315 participants in the workshops.

Summary

Recall that the total cost was $15,538. Compared with the total projected benefit in the first year of $820,776, we can see that the value of the benefits is 53 times greater than the costs. We have no reason to assume that the ability of managers to run shorter and fewer meetings will end after the first year, but the training manager was content using the figures for one year as the payback period.

As to the cost per student-hour, 315 employees attended the 6.5-hour workshop for a total of 2,047.5 student-hours. Dividing the total cost by the total number of student-hours gives us a cost per student-hour of $7.59. Notice that the total population to be trained included 95 managers and 250 employees. All of these persons attend meetings. However, they did not all attend the one-day workshop. Thus, the costs of training are based on the total number who attended (15×21, or 315), whereas the benefits of training were realized by all those who attend meetings (95 plus 250, or 345). There were undoubtedly other employees who also spend time in meetings, since Southwest Industries has about 900 employees, but they were not surveyed since their participation in meetings was seen as much less frequent.

CHAPTER 23

EVALUATING THE INSTRUCTOR

Upon completing this chapter you should be able to

◆ state the pros and cons of instructor evaluation by participants

◆ describe three tools for evaluating instructors professionally

◆ list at least eight criteria for instructor evaluation

◆ give several criteria that can best be evaluated by a professional

◆ indicate what should be done with instructor evaluation data.

Training programs are delivered either by a live instructor or by methods and media that are instructor independent (computer-based training, programmed learning, interactive video, distance learning). This chapter deals with the evaluation of the instructor, while the next chapter examines the design of the training program.

Neither of these evaluations is found on the Kirkpatrick four-level model. However, many organizations collect data on the professional quality of instructors and courses. Often an independent, respected outside professional is brought in as consultant to conduct these evaluations, although larger organizations may have the internal expertise and objectivity to evaluate and to recommend improvements.

Level 1 evaluations (reactions) can tell you whether participants liked the instructor. This is based on pacing, degree of participation, credibility, clarity of communications, and, of course, personality. But participants are not qualified to evaluate an instructor on such factors as appropriate wording of questions (directive vs. nondirective), inductive vs. deductive strategies, setting the learning contract, building transfer of training techniques into each lesson, eliciting relevant responses, or keeping the stimulus-response-feedback links in the instructional chain short (average: eight minutes). Hence the need for independent professional evaluation. Following are three means of evaluating instructors:

◆ Script for analysis—participants analyze the script of an instructor who is leading a discussion that takes place immediately after a role play.

◆ Interactive video—participants observe an instructor teaching a class on a video screen and respond to multiple-choice questions.

◆ Live classroom observation—evaluator observes a class, records observations, and gives instructor feedback.

This chapter contains tools illustrating the latter two methods: (a) the Trainer's Assessment of Proficiency (TAP) program, which includes a description of 12 competencies and skills; and (b) tools that an evaluator can use to record observations and give feedback: an instructor critique sheet (12 items) and an instructional skills assessment (48 items).

Trainer's Assessment of Proficiency (TAP): Twelve Instructional Competencies

1. **Assessing needs and entering behavior.** Before giving training, instructors must assess the needs, both organizational and individual, that they are expected to meet. The entering behavior of trainees (existing levels of knowledge, attitudes, and skills) is not at the level needed to perform their jobs with excellence. Hence the need for training.

2. **Setting objectives and terminal behavior.** At the start of a course, the instructor should announce the learning objectives. These statements describe the behaviors expected of participants during training and back on the job. Course objectives should be measurable, criterion-referenced, and relevant.

3. **Analyzing participants and situations.** Effective instructors can size up participants and situations so as to deal with them effectively in class. An understanding of human behavior and sensitivity to wording and actions is central to this competency.

4. **Eliciting relevant responses and testing.** Instructors need feedback from participants so as to assess learning and understanding. Participants need opportunities to think about new concepts and procedures, and to apply them to their own situation. Both of these needs are met when an instructor elicits responses that are (a) relevant to the objectives, and (b) calculated to show application and not merely acquisition of new concepts and terms.

5. **Applying classroom facilitation skills.** This competency is concerned with all the actions an instructor can take to maintain a classroom climate of openness, trust, and learning through participation and shared experience. Facilitation skills include the ability to lead discussion, summarize, probe, steer, maintain an appropriate pace, use visuals effectively, and act as a catalyst for group learning.

6. **Forming questions and probes effectively.** The question may well be an instructor's most useful tool. When teaching inductively (lecture method), questions are needed to test for understanding. When teaching deductively (Socratic method), questions are used to elicit information, experience, and insights from participants. And

probes are used to follow up on questions when we want participants to go into further depth without being prompted (and possibly biased) by further questions from us.

7. **Maintaining adult relationships (not parent-to-child).** Throughout our public schooling, the predominant relationship between teachers and learners has been a parent-to-child one. Students were dependent on teachers—for approval, for grades, for knowing what we needed to learn, and why. Although the classroom in corporate America should be conducted on an adult-to-adult basis (interdependence), instructors frequently lapse, often unconsciously, into filling a parent role and treating participants as children.

8. **Giving feedback and reinforcement.** Whenever participants respond, they should receive immediate feedback on the appropriateness of the response. This reinforcement confirms understanding and increases the probability that the participant will perform correctly following class. In a parent-to-child classroom, the feedback usually comes from the teacher or the textbook [answers in the back]. But with adult learners, feedback can come from fellow participants working in subgroups or from the nature of the assignment or task.

9. **Building toward transfer of training.** New concepts and skills acquired in class are like fragile seedlings nurtured in a greenhouse. They need to be transplanted into the soil of the workplace and helped to take root. This is a major difference between training and education: Trainers have a responsibility (and many opportunities in class) to help trainees transfer their new learning into action back on the job.

10. **Getting all learners to participate.** In most training programs, the "20/80 rule" is alive and well. The same 20% of the participants can be counted on to give 80% of the answers. Since people learn best by participating, however, the effective instructor must plan ways to elicit responses from all participants. When we pose a question in class and call on the first person to raise a hand, we may unwittingly be short-circuiting the learning process in all the other participants. They immediately shut down their thinking and listen for an answer that they've not had time to formulate for themselves.

11. **Managing classroom time effectively.** A lesson plan is the tool instructors use to manage their time in class. Time estimates can be written in the margin. These reminders help the instructor to know when to pick up the pace and when to make tradeoffs between one exercise and another. Letting the class know how much time has been allocated for each activity is also helpful.

12. **Displaying good flow, logic, and organization.** This last competency measures your analytical thinking skills and your ability to look at the design of a course and the behavior of an instructor with a view toward purpose and effect. Is it appropriate? Will it work? How will participants react? Are there more effective alternatives? The professional instructor is always looking for ways to improve the design and delivery of a course.

INSTRUCTOR CRITIQUE SHEET

Class given by: _____

On the topic: _____

How effective was the instructor in satisfying each of the following criteria? Place an X in the column that applies.

	Excellent	Good	Average	Inadequate	Poor/Omitted
1. Making the topic and objectives (what and why) clear at the start of the class					
2. Establishing the need and the level of understanding (entering behavior) of participants					
3. Breaking up the information input (S) so as to get responses (R) that measure understanding					
4. Eliciting relevant responses from all participants and not just the verbal minority					
5. Giving immediate and sufficient feedback to learners (F) so as to confirm or correct their understanding					
6. Maintaining an appropriate balance between input and output (acquisition-demonstration-application)					
7. Using the flipchart, board, overhead projector, or other audiovisual aids appropriately					
8. Using handouts appropriately (reference materials, job aid, flowcharts, hands-on exercises, demonstrations, tests)					
9. Creating and maintaining student interest via good pacing, via wording, analogies, delivery, humor					
10. Summarizing and giving closure to the class so that it ends on a positive note of high impact and commitment					
11. Managing time effectively (avoiding spending too much or too little time on parts of the class; sticking to schedule)					
12. Preparing and following an outline that served as an appropriate road map for the journey					
	4	3	2	1	0

Directions for scoring: Add up the number of Xs in each column, then multiply by the value indicated to the right, to get the final score in each column. The sum of these five scores indicates the overall effectiveness of the instructor. Out of a possible perfect score of 48, this instructor earned a score of ☐

Additional comments, suggestions, reactions:

INSTRUCTIONAL SKILLS ASSESSMENT

This self-assessment exercise is designed to give instructors a better view of their strengths and weaknesses in class. There are 48 statements. Each is followed by a box in which you or your rater (if someone else is evaluating you) should assign a number as follows:

5 Excellent; top rating; no improvement needed.

4 Good; but could be better with practice.

3 Average; needs some coaching on this.

2 Below average; much coaching and practice needed.

1 Poor; did not demonstrate this skill at all.

After completing the ratings on each of the 48 statements, follow the instructions for interpreting the results, printed below. If you are scoring yourself, do not read below this line until you have completed your ratings.

Instructions for interpreting the results. Each of the six columns addresses a different dimension of instructional skills. The six dimensions are described below:

Column one (items 1-8) deals with the instructor's role as a catalyst and facilitator and mediator of learning.

Column two (items 9-16) deals with the instructor's ability to teach on an adult-to-adult basis and not become "parent."

Column three (items 17-24) deals with the instructor's ability to keep a good balance between stimulus-response-feedback.

Column four (items 25-32) deals with the instructor's organizational skills in pacing and managing the instructional sequence.

Column five (items 33-40) deals with the instructor's ability to teach effectively in both the inductive and deductive modes.

Column six (items 41-48) deals with the instructor's effectiveness as a communicator.

Total of the six boxes

With a maximum of five points possible on each of the eight items in each column, the total score in each of our six dimensions is 40. Similarly, the total possible on the entire exercise is 240. Enter your totals in the boxes at the bottom of each column. Then add these six scores to obtain your overall total. Enter all of these scores in the boxes provided on this page. A score of 200 or better indicates an instructor who is generally proficient, although there may be strengths in some areas and weaknesses in others. Thus, it is important to assess the individual column scores as well as the total.

1. Elicits responses with ease; does not have to work hard to get the group to answer. ❑	**9.** Treats participants as adult learners and avoids becoming parent (judge, nurturer). ❑
2. Uses chalkboard (flipchart) to record and stimulate further thought. ❑	**10.** Sets the pace according to the group's need and ability to move. ❑
3. Reinforces participants for their contributions, thereby increasing participation. ❑	**11.** Draws on the experience and functions of participants to illustrate points. ❑
4. Avoids biasing the group by drawing on his or her own experience. ❑	**12.** Maintains a good balance between small group and full group activities. ❑
5. Maintains a high level of interest; participants are stimulated and active. ❑	**13.** Makes learning objectives known up front ("The purpose of this next exercise …"). ❑
6. Remains sensitive and responsive to needs of the group and its members. ❑	**14.** Facilitates the exchange of experience, so participants can learn from one another. ❑
7. Uses a variety of techniques to promote and stimulate interaction. ❑	**15.** Lets the group evaluate inappropriate behavior rather than having to play the judge role. ❑
8. Relates new contributions to earlier ones; gets discussion going among others. ❑	**16.** Leads participants to translate in class how they will perform back on the job. ❑

❑ ❑

17. Maintains a learner-centered focus, with much dialog and interaction. ❑

18. Keeps appropriate balance between content and process, between stimulus and responses. ❑

19. Asks questions that elicit appropriate and relevant responses. ❑

20. Maintains stimulus control: one point, handout at a time; controls distractions. ❑

21. Breaks big stimuli (more than five to six minutes) into smaller SRF links to get response. ❑

22. Gets all participants forming responses before calling on one or two. ❑

23. Uses techniques to give everyone feedback on their own responses (dyads, triads). ❑

24. Calls on other participants to evaluate the appropriateness of a given response. ❑

25. Manages time effectively, controls digressions, and keeps to the schedule. ❑

26. Checks out and controls: room temperature, refreshments, seating, audiovisual equipment. ❑

27. Refers back to learning objectives periodically to see how well they are being met. ❑

28. Handles interruptions, hidden agendas, irrelevancies, so as to stay on target. ❑

29. Obtains closure at appropriate points with summary statements and wrap-ups. ❑

30. Uses connective explanations to provide flow and sense of continuity to workshop. ❑

31. Reinforces importance of action plan by referring to it throughout workshop exercises. ❑

32. Makes learning objectives of each activity known at the start of the activity. ❑

❑ ❑

33. Uses inductive instructional strategies appropriately, with enough time in acquisition-demonstration-application. ❑

34. Applies probes and nondirective questions to shape and draw out the desired responses. ❑

35. Elicits illustrations and examples from the experience of the group to make a point. ❑

36. Rephrases questions to increase understanding and give more thinking time so all can deduce. ❑

37. Leads participants to discover and work out the consequences of their responses. ❑

38. Avoids fishing trips ("That's true, but it's not what I'm thinking," or "I have two more …"). ❑

39. Teaches deductively whenever it's easier to build on the learner's high entering behavior. ❑

40. Maintains a good balance of inductive and deductive techniques, using each effectively. ❑

41. Uses concrete, simple language; avoids jargon or abstract or imprecise language. ❑

42. Uses visuals spontaneously (chalkboard or flipchart) to bring a point to life. ❑

43. Employs full range of vocal dynamics (pitch, rate, articulation, inflection) to keep interest high. ❑

44. Uses good examples, analogies, and illustrations to clarify points and dramatize the message. ❑

45. Makes effective use of humor, levity, informality, and human interest. ❑

46. Gives complete, concise, clear, crisp instructions when making assignments. ❑

47. Provides topic headings and labels to help participants organize the message more meaningfully. ❑

48. Has good stage presence; words, manners, gestures, and body language all work together effectively. ❑

❑   ❑

CHAPTER 24

CRITERIA FOR SELECTING AND EVALUATING COURSE DESIGN

Upon completing this chapter you should be able to

◆ state why evaluation criteria must precede make or buy decisions

◆ list at least eight course design criteria

◆ give a half-dozen benefits of making and of buying courses

◆ apply the Instructional Design Checklist to your course(s), with calculations

◆ indicate what kinds of courses you would make? you would buy?

Whether you make or buy training courses, you need to establish the criteria to be used in evaluating them. The Kirkpatrick four-level model is concerned with evaluations taken after the training has been conducted. Our concern here is with evaluation before you run a course—perhaps even before you design or purchase it, if this is an option.

To be sure, the ultimate measure of effectiveness is the performance of trainees and the organization following training. By evaluating beforehand and taking appropriate action, however, we can increase the potential impact and the probability of improved effectiveness. Put more simply, the quality of the course design correlates with the quality of the learner's performance after training. This is why courses should be evaluated in advance of being scheduled. Fortunately, there are a number of well-established criteria. Forewarned is forearmed. Here are a few examples of the evaluation criteria:

◆ Are objectives stated? As outcomes (workplace behavior, not academic)?

◆ Is message at a level appropriate to audience (relevance, entering behavior)?

◆ Are course materials attractive? Meaty? User-friendly? Current?

◆ Is interaction sufficient? Balanced (input-output, stimulus-response)?

◆ Are learning exercises well designed? Appropriate? Time-effective?

◆ Is cost reasonable and affordable relative to benefits?

◆ Are procedures to maximize transfer of training built in?

◆ Are responsibilities of three parties spelled out (trainer-trainee-boss)?

◆ Are detailed guidelines provided for instructor and administrator?

◆ Have evaluation tools been provided? Do they measure the desired behavior?

◆ Has the course been field tested and validated?

This chapter contains two tools that you should find useful: a make or buy checklist and the Instructional Design Checklist. The scores on each will help you pinpoint areas of strength and weakness in the instructional design.

Make or Buy

Thirty years ago the "make or buy" question was seldom raised: Trainers had to make the courses they taught. To be sure, there were training films available on a variety of subjects. But packaged courses containing participant workbooks, instructor guidelines, audiovisual support material, handouts, tests, and job aids had not yet arrived on the scene. Today training managers can scan a half-dozen directories that describe the thousands of training programs now available.

In the past, course development was largely synonymous with the writing of a training manual. The result was a heavy binder crammed with policy, procedures, and reprints. The reading level was difficult, illustrations and white space were virtually unheard of, and audiovisual support (if any) referred to overhead transparencies and flipchart pages. An electronic age has enabled trainers to use methods and media that are far more effective in imparting information and in providing opportunities for learners to apply it: computer-based training, videocassettes, interactive video, PC-linked keypad response systems, touch-screen (info-window) video. Today's trainees have been raised on TV and the PC. They expect technology in the classroom and in self-study programs. And the effectiveness of the new electronic methods and media, when used appropriately in an instructional design, cannot be disputed.

The challenge facing training managers is great. Thirty years ago, the average cost of a course per-trainee-per-hour was well under $5 (excluding salary and facilities). Today this figure is much higher because it's a lot more expensive to produce videotapes and computer software than it is to write a training manual. Thus, the make or buy decision is more critical than ever.

The next two pages contain 10 statements that support "make" and 10 that favor "buy." This exercise can be thought of as a decision matrix. The next time you are faced with a make or buy decision, assign a value to each statement to reflect its relative importance. We suggest using a four-point scale, as follows: 3 = extremely important; 2 = somewhat important; 1 = slightly important; and 0 = not relevant.

Benefits of Developing Your Own Courses

1. The content and objectives are unique to your organization and cannot be purchased as a packaged course. ❑

2. You have skilled writers, media experts, and course designers on staff and want to take advantage of their talent. ❑

3. Your audience of trainees will assign more credibility and relevance to training if it is developed internally. ❑

4. Your management expects you to create training programs rather than purchase them in packaged form. ❑

5. You don't have the budget to purchase courses, and the payroll costs of developing them is not viewed as an expense. ❑

6. The large number of trainees in your target audience makes the cost per person of packaged courses prohibitively high. ❑

7. The course content will need frequent updating, which is easier to handle when you own the course. ❑

8. Some firms that supply packaged courses require licensing of instructors, which you feel is expensive and unnecessary. ❑

9. You've examined the packaged course(s) and would have to make too many modifications to meet your learning objectives. ❑

10. It's a policy of your organization to develop your own training rather than purchase it from outside sources. ❑

Total score favoring development of your own courses ❑

Benefits of Purchasing a Packaged Course

1. The content and objectives of the available courses fit our needs; why reinvent the wheel? ❏

2. The quality of graphics and audiovisual material is superior to what we can produce ourselves. ❏

3. We cannot afford professional talent of the caliber used to create the packaged courses. ❏

4. Success on the initial offerings is more likely with a program that has a proven track record. ❏

5. The course objectives are more likely to be achieved on a packaged course that has been field tested and validated. ❏

6. By using packaged courses where they fit, your development time is free to create courses that you must design (they don't exist). ❏

7. Because the supplier's developmental expense is spread over a number of clients, your cost is usually less than developing a course yourself. ❏

8. A support network exists: other clients, the supplier's staff, consultants who teach the course. ❏

9. The quality of delivery is maintained through detailed instructor guidelines, train-the-trainer workshops, user's conferences. ❏

10. It's more cost effective to buy a course if it fits your needs and criteria by 70% or better. (You can always develop or modify the other 30% yourself.) ❏

Total score favoring the purchase of a packaged course ❏

INSTRUCTIONAL DESIGN CHECKLIST

This exercise is designed to help you identify and evaluate the impact of 50 factors that contribute to the effectiveness of an instructional system. These factors are arranged under 10 headings, as noted below. Five factors contribute to each. The checklist can be used proactively (before designing or selecting a course) or reactively (evaluating an existing course).

If you are in the process of designing an instructional system, this checklist can help you to build into the development or selection process those actions that can best contribute to the effectiveness and impact of the course. If you are in the process of evaluating the design of an existing instructional system that you have been using, this checklist can help you assess the presence of a number of factors that are important to the program's impact.

Here's how the checklist works. Each of the 50 items is followed by a three-point rating scale: 2-1-0. Your job is to circle the number that best describes your evaluation of the factor. Here is their meaning:

2 Great. This factor is in good shape.
1 This factor is present, but needs some work.
0 Poor. This factor is absent or needs much work.

After evaluating the 50 factors, add up the totals under each of the 10 headings. Then enter these ratings in the boxes that follow the 10 headings, listed below. A rating of 10 points is the best score you can obtain on each heading. Thus, a rating of 100 points is the maximum possible as your overall instructional design score.

1. Needs analysis and definition of the problem or purpose ❏

2. Behavioral objectives for the course ❏

3. Subject matter and course content ❏

4. Methods, media, strategies, and instructional process ❏

5. Preparation of trainees prior to the course ❏

6. Application of an adult learning model ❏

7. Follow-up, transfer, and maintenance of performance at work ❏

8. Evaluation, validation, and revision ❏

9. Instructor's effectiveness ❏

10. Logistics and administrative support ❏

Overall instructional design score ❏

Overall Instructional Design Score

1. Needs analysis and definition of the problem or purpose

(a) Performance criteria exist and have been approved by management.   2 1 0
(b) Pretraining performance measures exist and document a real need.   2 1 0
(c) Performance gaps noted as knowledge, attitude, skill deficiencies.   2 1 0
(d) Workplace reinforcers (+) and constraints (–) have been identified.   2 1 0
(e) Purpose of training is linked to the business plan (organizational goals).   2 1 0

Total points under this heading

2. Behavioral objectives for the course

(a) Objectives exist and serve as blueprint for course design or selection.   2 1 0
(b) Course objectives are measurable and describe learning outcomes.   2 1 0
(c) Objectives state workshop and workplace behaviors (expectations).   2 1 0
(d) Trainees and supervisors get objectives before course as a "contract."   2 1 0
(e) Instructor checks for attainment of objectives throughout course.   2 1 0

Total points under this heading

3. Subject matter and course content

(a) Content relates directly to objectives (lean meat, no fat).   2 1 0
(b) Appropriate examples, illustrations, analogies bring content to life.   2 1 0
(c) Content is presented in a crisp, complete, compelling manner.   2 1 0
(d) Level of instruction (verbal, conceptual) is appropriate to trainees.   2 1 0
(e) Design (format) allows for easy updating of content over time.   2 1 0

Total points under this heading

4. Methods, media, strategies, and instructional process

(a) Use of full group, subgroups, and self-study as appropriate.   2 1 0
(b) Balance between inductive and deductive strategies.   2 1 0
(c) Appropriate use of audiovisuals as input (video, slides, overheads).   2 1 0
(d) Appropriate use of audiovisuals as output (video recorder, flipchart, PC).   2 1 0
(e) Trainee's notebook and materials are designed for easy reference later.   2 1 0

Total points under this heading

5. Preparation of trainees prior to the course

(a) Precourse information sent to each trainee two to three weeks in advance.   2 1 0
(b) Each trainee meets with supervisor to discuss reasons for course.   2 1 0
(c) Trainees are given data to document the need (organizational and personal).   2 1 0
(d) Course begins with orientation or overview of purpose, expectations.   2 1 0
(e) Majority of trainees are glad to be attending (positive motivation).   2 1 0

Total points under this heading

6. Application of an adult learning model

(a)	Course is learner centered (not information or instructor centered).	2	1	0
(b)	Good balance in macro model: acquisition-demonstration-application.	2	1	0
(c)	Small bites in micro model: stimulus-response-feedback (8-min. average).	2	1	0
(d)	Sufficient and work-related opportunity for hands-on practice.	2	1	0
(e)	Trainees learn much from one another, not just from the instructor.	2	1	0

Total points under this heading

7. Follow-up, transfer, and maintenance of performance at work

(a)	Supervisors are prepared to recognize and reinforce new behavior.	2	1	0
(b)	Trainees take job aids back to workplace (checklists, action plans).	2	1	0
(c)	Instructors periodically visit workplace and get feedback.	2	1	0
(d)	Forms and procedures exist for giving trainees feedback on the job.	2	1	0
(e)	Supervisors and instructors meet to strengthen course's impact.	2	1	0

Total points under this heading

8. Evaluation, validation, and revision

(a)	Workshop expectations (Levels 1 and 2) are measured in the classroom.	2	1	0
(b)	Workplace expectations (Levels 3 and 4) are measured back on the job.	2	1	0
(c)	Data from (a) and (b) are used to refine and strengthen the course.	2	1	0
(d)	Pilot cycles are measured with extra rigor to ensure course validity.	2	1	0
(e)	Evaluation data is summarized and shared with management.	2	1	0

Total points under this heading

9. Instructor's effectiveness

(a)	Instructor knows subject and has credibility in trainee's eyes.	2	1	0
(b)	Class is participative with instructor as catalyst and facilitator.	2	1	0
(c)	Preclass preparation (of self, trainees, materials, facilities).	2	1	0
(d)	Postcourse follow-up (put away, documentation, maintenance).	2	1	0
(e)	Instructor receives good ratings from trainees at end of course.	2	1	0

Total points under this heading

10. Logistics and administrative support

(a)	Life cycle of course and number of offerings have been estimated.	2	1	0
(b)	Length of course and frequency of offerings are appropriate.	2	1	0
(c)	Locations and facilities are selected and appropriate.	2	1	0
(d)	Group size and criteria for enrollment are effective.	2	1	0
(e)	Trainers receive needed administrative support from management.	2	1	0

Total points under this heading

CHAPTER 25

PUBLICIZING YOUR SUCCESS

Upon completing this chapter you should be able to

◆ list at least four useful actions for publicizing your success

◆ state the five major audiences you need to reach

◆ describe the information that should go into a success story

◆ describe how you plan to promote your course's success.

All too often training is seen as an expense—a cost of doing business. If we can evaluate its impact and prove that our courses more than pay their own way, we are less likely to suffer budget cuts in hard times and more likely to get money and support to launch new programs and maintain existing ones. However, you're probably going to have to publicize your success to win the support you deserve. Once you have carried out the appropriate evaluations described in the preceding chapters you have a data bank and are armed to promote the cause. As Gilbert and Sullivan put it in their operetta "Ruddigore":

> *If you wish in the world to advance,*
> *Your merits you're bound to enhance,*
> *You must stir it and stump it,*
> *And blow your own trumpet,*
> *Or, trust me, you haven't a chance!*

Let's examine a list of actions you might consider as a means of winning support and getting a return on the investment you made in evaluating courses and analyzing data:

◆ Prepare a report (success story with data) for senior management.

◆ Send out a congratulatory memo to graduates and their managers.

◆ Write a success story for the employee newsletter or house organ.

◆ Have public relations people include several paragraphs in the annual report.

◆ Submit a story to a training journal, trade publication, or local newspaper.

◆ Circulate reprints of any articles you manage to get printed.

◆ Prepare a cost-benefit analysis and share it with senior management.

◆ Have trainees give you a postcourse memo documenting its impact on them.

Who are the audiences you need to reach with a story that outlines the success of your course? Here are the major ones:

◆ **Employees who are potential trainees.** Their attitude toward the course will be much more positive if they see quotes of graduates who have endorsed the training as a valuable experience.

◆ **Supervisors who enroll their people** and release them from work to attend class. They need to hear that time in class is time invested rather than time spent.

◆ **Managers who approve budgets** for training. They want to know what the return on investment has been for training in general and your course in particular. (Our failure to provide this data in the past has sometimes led to cuts in the training budget in hard times.)

◆ **Your own supervisor** wants to see all these audiences supportive of training, and should be your editor in reviewing your first draft.

◆ **Your fellow professionals** in the field of training. An article in one of the national training journals will help your own growth and development.

The following is a reprint of a success story reporting the results of a training program: "Supervisory Training at Lenox Hill." More than 300 supervisors and managers went through the eight-session Challenge of Management program. This article, prepared by Joan Holland, the hospital's training director, appeared in *Cross-Reference,* the monthly newsletter of the American Hospital Association. Of particular interest is the design of the training, with one session per week and meetings during the interim between the participants and their managers. Following the course, the supervisors formed the Middle Management Association that meets 10 times a year for ongoing growth and development.

Supervisory Training at Lenox Hill

by Joan S. Holland,
Training Director,
Lenox Hill Hospital,
New York City

"We had not run a management development program at the hospital for years," explains William A. Lockom, director of personnel. "The program was needed to develop supervisory skills, strengthen any weaknesses, develop interaction among various professional and paraprofessional groups, and create understanding of health care and the operation of a hospital. We looked outside the hospital for a firm or individual who could assist us in setting up and conducting the first cycles of the course and finally chose the "Challenge of Management" program offered by Training House.

"Whenever we use materials created by an outside group, there is a danger that the program will be perceived as a 'canned' course and less relevant than a 'home grown' product that was developed internally. That has not been our experience; in fact, I think we gained the best of both worlds."

The course is based on learning through participation because participants learn best not by being told, but by experiencing the consequences of their actions. Thus, there are no lectures. Instead, the classroom becomes a laboratory where supervisors and managers try out new concepts, skills, and procedures through the use of case discussions, role plays, games and simulations, self-inventory exercises, and other forms of interactive learning. Participants find this more interesting as well as more relevant to the day-to-day problems they face.

To increase the impact of the program, it was tailored to the specific needs of the hospital. For example, before launching the course we administered a survey of the organization climate to all participants and their department heads. Each participant received a profile with an analysis of what that profile meant. This survey indicated that each stratum of management had different feelings about the hospital and that top management needed to clarify its goals to other management personnel and improve working relationships among departments.

The data produced by this survey and other assessment exercises administered throughout the early weeks of the course gave us a good understanding of organizational needs and the personal needs of employees.

Between classes, each participant met with the department head or assistant administrator to complete exercises that required their joint effort. This helped to break down any communication gap that may exist between first-level supervisors and their bosses.

Each participant also was asked to prepare a behavioral, performance-oriented job description as an ongoing assignment during the course. With each new topic, the participants prepared a new entry indicating: a) how they planned to apply the concepts, skills and procedures they had just acquired; and b) what goals or performance criteria they wanted to be evaluated against by their manager or assistant administrator. These new entries were then checked with the appropriate department head or assistant administrator during the weekly partnership meetings.

One of the most interesting aspects of the course occurred toward its end. The consultant and I suggested to the participants that they might wish to form a supervisory association and continue to meet on a voluntary basis. As the consultant explained, one of the characteristics of a professional is the desire to share knowledge and to continue one's personal growth by learning from one another. If supervisors and line managers are expected to behave professionally, they should have a forum for the sharing of ideas, experiences, and new concepts. Growth is an ongoing affair; it doesn't start and stop in the classroom.

The participants expressed interest but wondered whether the administrators would be in favor of the idea. "After all," a nursing supervisor reminded the class, "such an association might be seen as a move toward unionization or at least as another group whose collective voice might have to be listened to. I don't know if the president of the hospital would go for that."

As it turned out, David A. Reed, president of Lenox Hill Hospital, did go for the idea. "Managing a hospital is a team effort," he explained. "We need all the help we can get. I can't think of another industry that is harder hit by the crunch of fixed prices and rising costs. Hospitals are the most labor-intensive enterprises in society today, with employees often outnumbering bed patients by more than three to one. This means that effective supervision at all levels is imperative if the quality of our service is not to suffer. In the past, we've often tended to overlook the importance of our supervisors and first-level managers. Like the shoemaker's children, we were so busy tending the needs of our patients that we neglected our own development. The implementation of our supervisory skills development program is a start in changing that direction.

"As for the decision by the 60 graduates of the first cycle of the program to form a Lenox Hill Middle Management Association, I'm delighted that they are interested in furthering their growth and extending to others the benefits they've obtained from participating in the course. The other administrators and I look forward to this development and are sure that we can build a stronger management development team at Lenox Hill as a result."

The Middle Management Association meets 10 times a year and includes all graduates of the program. Members have adopted a constitution and have elected officers. At the meetings, programs are presented that enlarge members' knowledge of hospital operation and management skills. Mr. Reed also has sought the assistance of the group in solving specific problems within the hospital.

How effective has the supervisory skills development program been in improving the skills of supervisors? This question can be answered best by the department heads who sent their staff to the course and met with them during the weekly partnership meetings. One department head said: "Initially, I had a rather negative attitude about the course, especially when I found that one of my best supervisors had been enrolled in the course. I wondered what the course could possibly teach her that would be worth the lost time and disruption that her attendance would mean to our department. I went along reluctantly with her participation. However, as the program ran its course, I was able to see how much she was getting out of it. I believe we both benefited from that dialog."

Another measure of the program's effectiveness comes from the evaluations turned in. Some of the more representative responses were:

- "The critical incidents gave me ideas on how others handle problems and let me know that I wasn't the only one with problems."

- "We acted out roles and saw the reactions of others to our comments and gestures. I didn't realize I came across that way and know that I have to be more careful."

- "I learned quite a bit about the union and hope to regard it no longer as an enemy. The union organizer is like me—a manager in the middle."

- "It has given me many insights into my methods of dealing with employees and my relations with management."

At present, the fifth cycle of 60 participants is nearing completion. I learned a great deal from team-teaching the first cycle with the consultant and now feel comfortable teaching the course alone. Only time will tell what long-term impact the program will have but one thing is certain—we're off to a good start!

CHAPTER 26

EVALUATING YOUR INSTRUCTIONAL COMPETENCIES

Upon completing this chapter you should be able to

◆ identify the six competencies assessed by the ACID test

◆ indicate your greatest strengths and weaknesses on the six

◆ define the inductive and deductive modes of instruction

◆ give examples of parent-to-child and adult-to-adult behavior in class

◆ distinguish between the macro (ADA) and micro (SRF) models of learning

◆ illustrate ADA with examples from your own course(s).

In chapter 23 we examined some of the criteria and methods for evaluating instructors. Perhaps you are an instructor or work with instructors, in which case this chapter will be of particular interest. It contains a self-assessment created by Training House, Inc., and reproduced by permission: the Assessment of Competencies for Instructor Development (the ACID test). This exercise is designed to measure your relative strength in the underlying skills that are important to the success of a trainer. Since we are concerned with measuring your skills and attitudes (values, opinions) rather than your knowledge, the items contained in this test are situational in nature. That is, most of them present a specific situation and ask how you would deal with it.

There are 30 items in this assessment. Each is followed by four choices. Your job is to pick those choices that indicate how you would respond to the situation. After you have done so, check your answers against ours. You may pick more than one response from each set of four choices.

The ACID Test

1. You've been asked to teach a workshop on effective business writing. To find out the needs of your participants, you've decided to send out an assignment in advance, to be returned one week before the workshop. Which of the following will you use?

   A. "Select and critique a recent letter that is representative of your writing."

   B. "Edit the enclosed letter with red pen, then rewrite it."

   C. "Answer this 12-item questionnaire about your writing needs."

   D. "Indicate the relevance of the enclosed learning objectives to your needs."

2. A friend of yours is a trainer in a department store, where she teaches new sales assistants. Four of her learning objectives are listed below. You plan to tell her that her best objectives state that "upon completing the course, the sales assistants will be able to:

   A. Describe the correct procedure for dealing with a customer complaint.

   B. Demonstrate via role play at least two ways of handling returns.

   C. Understand the importance of following correct security procedures.

   D. Follow a five-step procedure for making change."

3. Xanadu Corporation is running a training program to teach its sales people eight techniques for closing a sale. They now want to measure the course's effectiveness. They should probably consider the following test(s) of effectiveness:

   A. Script analysis: On scripts of calls, trainees indicate when and how to close.

   B. True-false test: Trainees answer 20 statements on dos and don'ts of closing.

   C. Matching: Trainees pair up names of techniques with an example of each.

   D. Role play: Trainees try to sell to person playing the customer role.

4. In the course that will be launched next week, a new policy will be introduced along with forms needed for its implementation. Management suspects that this policy and its forms will be unpopular with participants. Your best way of teaching it is to introduce the policy and then:

   A. Explain how the forms work, stressing why the policy is necessary.

   B. Have the class generate pros and cons, which you record on a flipchart.

   C. Break into subgroups to discuss the policy's benefits and drawbacks.

D. Tell them you realize it is unpopular, but that in the long run the reasons for it will outweigh the present negative feelings.

5. While instructing you notice that two of your participants are talking to one another again for the second time in the past 10 minutes. It would be a good idea for you to:

A. Pause in silence until they stop talking and rejoin the group.

B. Pose a question and have the class discuss it in three-person groups.

C. Ask the two if what they're discussing is relevant.

D. Assume that it might be related to the lesson and continue instructing.

6. You are in the second day of a three-day course and are seriously behind schedule. This group of trainees is slower than past groups—they interrupt your lectures with simple questions and require more time to grasp the basics. So you decide to:

A. Leave out much of the remaining course content and focus on basics.

B. Ask for their help if you're to cover everything and keep to schedule.

C. Give shorter lectures and provide questions for subgroup discussions.

D. Ask them to hold their questions until the end of each lecture.

7. In presenting a workshop on time management, you've decided that the best way to spend the first 10 minutes of the workshop (after the introductions and administrative details) would be to:

A. Generate in subgroups a list of time robbers in the workplace.

B. Give the group an overview of the course design and content.

C. Have participants describe their biggest frustrations in managing time.

D. Outline the major barriers to effective time management.

8. Indicate your rating of these course objectives, taken from the part of a technical training program that deals with measurement. "Upon completing this lesson, the trainee will be able to:

A. Indicate how a vernier caliper and a micrometer work.

B. Measure the inside and outside diameter of three sizes of pipes.

C. Determine the size of a coin and a steel ball to .001mm accuracy.

D. Describe the three parts of a micrometer and the functions of each."

9. John is designing a half-day writing skills course for correspondents in the policy inquiries section of an insurance company. He plans to use four activities: (a) examples of poorly written letters that participants edit or rewrite; (b) an amusing film showing how differently a reader can interpret what the writer meant; (c) a lecture with

demonstrations on the dos and don'ts of good writing; and (d) sample inquiries from customers (policyholders) to be answered. You tell John that the best sequence(s) of these activities might be:

A. First (b) then (a) then (d). Eliminate (c).

B. First (c) then (a) then (d). Eliminate (b).

C. First (b) then (c) then (a) then (d).

D. First (c) then (d) then (a). End with (b).

10. Suppose you are teaching a technical course to 20 newly hired employees, four of whom are experienced and usually answer correctly while the others find the material new and difficult. Thus, much of your teaching should be:

A. Inductive lecture directed mainly to the inexperienced new hires.

B. Deductive discussion with the more experienced responding more often.

C. Deductive exercises done in subgroups that mix experience levels.

D. Inductive, with questions directed to those who volunteer to answer.

11. One of your participants, Joe, is writing a memo or report during your lecture. You should probably:

A. Check to see if other participants are becoming disinterested.

B. Pose a question and call on Joe for the answer.

C. Continue lecturing but look at Joe until he rejoins you.

D. Intersperse some questions and learner activity into your lecture.

12. You are scheduled to teach selection interviewing to a group of trainees whose level of knowledge and experience is unknown to you. Given this situation, you might devote the first hour or so of class to a:

A. Script of an interview that they evaluate in subgroups, then report on.

B. Test to measure their knowledge of selection interviewing.

C. Lecture to establish the major steps in a good interview.

D. Discussion of the difficulties they've had when interviewing.

13. A friend of yours is designing a course on statistical process control (SPC) to help supervisors control quality on the production line. She wants your advice on how to start the course. You suggest that she open with a:

A. Brief overview of what SPC is and how it can help.

B. Simple explanation of normal distribution (median, mean, mode).

C. Short discussion of the quality control problems that trainees have faced.

D. Case study of a production problem of unacceptably high reject rate.

14. The main value in having a list of learning objectives for a course is that they can be used to:

    A. Inform participants and their managers in advance of the course.

    B. Ensure that the instructor stays on target and does not digress.

    C. Demonstrate that the course is learner centered and results oriented.

    D. Establish expectations and monitor progress toward them.

15. In using lecture method, a good rule of thumb is to:

    A. Stop every five to 10 minutes and pose a question for all trainees to answer.

    B. Announce at the start you will welcome questions at the end of the lecture.

    C. Ask periodically if people understand or if they have any questions.

    D. Have trainees turn to a neighbor and respond to every major learning point.

16. Participants in the five-day course, Basics of Supervision, have been supervising for an average of 18 months before attending. You decide that the course should probably be taught:

    A. By lecture wherever bad habits must be replaced by more effective ones.

    B. With films and videotapes that show only correct models.

    C. By discussion so people can identify what works from their own experience.

    D. With case method and role play and participants learning from one another.

17. You're in the midst of teaching a procedure when Art, one of your more outspoken participants, says: "That's nice in theory, but it just doesn't apply around here. It would never fly." You might:

    A. Explain that it has worked and will work if we want it to.

    B. Ask Art to hold his fire until you're finished and then discuss it.

    C. Probe to find out what barriers Art has in mind.

    D. Ask the class how they feel about Art's comment.

18. Training would be a lot more effective and trainees would perform better if instructors:

    A. Spent more time asking questions and testing for understanding.

    B. Organized their lectures better: flow, examples, illustrations, handouts.

    C. Knew their subject better and had more confidence and credibility.

    D. Gave learners more hands-on learning and less lecture and visuals.

19. You are doing a needs analysis prior to teaching supervisors how to conduct effective performance appraisals. In particular you want to find out:

    A. How the appraisal form affects the quality of the review.

    B. How many appraisals your participants have conducted (average).

    C. What factors keep managers from giving honest appraisals.

    D. Whether employees really want to be appraised and how appraisals have affected their performance.

20. Which of the following objectives are appropriate for a supervisory training program? "After completing the session dealing with motivation, the supervisors will be able to:

    A. Name the five levels of Maslow's 'needs hierarchy' and describe each.

    B. Motivate their employees to achieve higher levels of performance.

    C. Describe at least three actions they can take to improve motivation.

    D. Meet with employees to develop action plans for increased job satisfaction."

21. You are just starting the first hour of a workshop on time management. A good way to open is to ask participants:

    A. How many of you really know how you are spending your time?

    B. What percentage of your time is and isn't under your control?

    C. How much time do you actually work during a typical week?

    D. What are the two or three biggest wasters of your time at work?

22. You are teaching deductively and leading a discussion following the reading of a case study. Participants are not coming up with the right answers. To correct this you decide to:

    A. Rephrase your questions so as to elicit the desired answers.

    B. Tell people "That's not what I'm looking for" and ask someone else.

    C. Give them the correct answers so as not to get bogged down.

    D. Pursue wrong answers by asking additional questions.

23. Most all of your learners participate in class—except Nancy. This is the third day of the course and she hasn't contributed yet. Perhaps you should:

    A. Call on her, noting that "we haven't heard from you yet."

    B. Pair up participants to discuss an issue; listen in on Nancy.

    C. Ask during break if she's having any trouble with the course.

    D. Call on her to relate a point she made in talking with you during the break.

24. Elaine's computer systems course consists of lectures (classroom) followed by labs (practice at terminals). Her present group of trainees covers a wide range of abilities, which creates a problem

in the labs; some finish their assignments quickly, while others take forever. To correct this, Elaine might:

A. Spend more time in lecture before going into the lab.

B. Have several lab assistants circulating to give help as needed.

C. Have different assignments for faster and slower students.

D. Pair up stronger and weaker students and have them work in pairs.

25. The stock room employees in your chain of discount stores are responsible for putting the price on the merchandise when they restock the shelves and displays. But they've gotten sloppy about it, and the people at the cash registers often have to call for a price check. The manager has asked you to retrain them. You should probably:

A. Run a refresher course and go back to the basics.

B. Tell the manager that it's probably a motivational problem.

C. Find out if the deficiency is one of knowledge, attitudes, or skills.

D. Watch them at work to see what reinforcers and constraints are operating.

26. Tom's workshop on negotiation skills is described below in the course objectives he has given you. Indicate your rating of them to:

A. Cover 12 negotiation strategies and the plus and minus factors of each.

B. Practice at least three strategies during two role play negotiations.

C. Describe any five negotiation strategies and indicate when to use each.

D. Stress how your assumptions (win-win vs. win-lose) can affect outcomes.

27. Training films from outside commercial sources are usually most effective when they are shown:

A. Near the start of a class if they combine lecture and demonstration.

B. Near the end of a class since they are entertaining and challenging.

C. With several stopping points so trainees can discuss it in installments.

D. To provide variety and audiovisuals in the design of a course.

28. George is teaching a group of service mechanics how to read a new schematic diagram just developed. He is not as familiar with it as he'd like to be. Therefore, George should teach it via:

A. Deductive discussion so that the participants can pool their understanding.

B. Inductive lecture so as to cover the things he does understand.

C. The team approach, using the company's expert as his co-instructor.

D. Hands-on learning where the participants discover for themselves.

29. You've noticed that some participants always sit with their friends. When you ask people to work with their neighbor on a question or assignment, the discussion among friends is predictable and often superficial. To get greater depth and fresh ideas, you've decided to:

    A. Ask the group to sit with new neighbors at each session.

    B. Arrange seating for each class by moving their name tents.

    C. Speak privately to pairs you want to break up.

    D. Break into larger groups (three to four persons) when giving assignments.

30. You've just completed one part of your lecture and have moved on to a new topic when a participant asks a rather basic question about something you just covered. You might want to:

    A. Ask the other participants if they are having trouble understanding.

    B. Explain it again, using different wording, examples, or analogies.

    C. Explain you're now on a new topic but will go over the old one after class.

    D. Ask the person some questions to diagnose where they are having trouble.

Guidelines for Interpreting the ACID Test

The six competencies that are important to one's effectiveness as an instructor are the ability to:

◆ analyze the needs and entering behavior of the learner

◆ specify outcomes and terminal behavior for a course

◆ design instructional sequences and learning materials

◆ instruct in both the inductive and deductive modes

◆ maintain adult relationships (not parent-to-child) in class

◆ stay learner centered rather than information centered.

Our purpose here is to define the competencies, explain their relevance, and illustrate them by referring back to items in the test. Before defining these six competencies, let's make sure we understand that a competency is "a combination of related knowledge, attitudes, and skills that prepares us to act in appropriate and effective ways." The last two competencies listed above rely more heavily on your values (attitudes) than do the first four, which have a heavier input of knowledge and skills. Now let's look at each in turn.

Analyzing the needs and entering behavior of the learner. The effective instructor will find out as much as possible about the needs of learners before getting into the instruction. When possible this should be done before class since the results will influence the design of the program. When precourse assessment is not possible, then the initial exercise in class can serve to give the instructor information about the knowledge, attitudes, and skills that the students already possess, and the nature and scope of their needs, since it is the instructor's responsibility to make the course relevant to those needs.

In item 1, answers A and B will give the instructor a sample of each student's writing, which is a much better way of determining their strengths and weaknesses (needs) than is a survey (answers C and D) that may fail to tap a person's true needs (since people don't know what they don't know, and will respond by indicating what they want).

In item 7, answers A and C will tell the instructor what problems and needs face the students. Until this data is collected, the activities described in answers B and D are premature.

In item 13, answers A and B get into the subject matter of the course before finding out what problems the participants have faced and how familiar they are with quality control. Hence answers C and D are correct.

In item 19, answers B and C will serve to break the ice and establish the students' entering behavior. Answers A and D are irrelevant and could even sidetrack the main objective.

In item 25, we must recognize that many factors influence the performance of employees at work. They should be examined before jumping to the conclusion that training is needed. Answers C and D reflect this.

Specifying outcomes and terminal behaviors for the course. This competency is concerned with the ability to state course objectives in terms that are measurable and observable. They should spell out the expected performance you are looking for from the learner. Whenever possible, objectives should spell out the desired behavior that will occur on the job rather than in class (for example, "learner will be able to assemble and operate an automobile jack" rather than "learner will be able to name the parts of a jack and describe its operation"). Trainers call this the terminal behavior. The main value of course objectives is that they let participants and their managers know the expected outcomes. Objectives are a form of contract that enables the instructor and the student to establish expectations and monitor progress toward them.

On item 2, answers B and D are correct. These deal with behaviors we expect to see on the job. The verbs in answers A and C are less desirable: "to describe" is a classroom behavior and "to understand" can't be observed or measured.

On item 8, answers B and C are true measures of whether the student knows how to operate a micrometer and a caliper. Answers A and D merely talk about them. Sometimes an instructor must settle for verbal descriptions of the desired behavior (for example, in military training or where safety or security are at stake). But in this example, the instructor can have students take measurements in class. Thus, we do not have to settle for verbal descriptions from students. We can watch them measure the pipes (B) and the coin and steel ball (C).

Item 14 is a restatement of the paragraph you just read. Answers A and D are correct. While B and C are desirable, the sharing of course objectives cannot ensure that B and C will take place.

In item 20, two of the objectives describe the desired behavior of supervisors back on the job: answers C and D. Answer A is a classroom behavior, and answer B is a wish rather than an objective. It can't be measured or observed (Did you ever watch someone "motivating"?).

In item 26 we can immediately eliminate answers A and D since they describe instructor behavior rather than student outcomes. (It's the instructor who wants "to cover" and "to stress.") This leaves answers B and C as correct. Both are classroom behaviors, but this is appropriate when learners apply their skills in a wide variety of situations at work that make it difficult if not impossible to spell out the specific behavior you would like back on the job. This is the case in the teaching of negotiation skills.

Designing instructional sequences and learning materials. The ability to design instructional sequences and materials is important to success as an instructor. Whether you create the courses you teach or acquire them ready for delivery to your students, you must be able to apply the three-stage learning model in shaping the behavior of students. These stages are acquisition (where we tell the learner new information), demonstration (where we show how the new information applies via examples, illustrations, or cases), and application (where we give learners a hands-on chance to apply what they've just acquired).

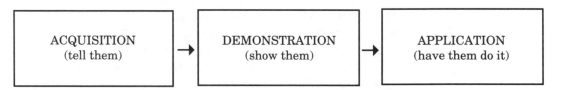

The acquisition-demonstration-application (ADA) model gives us a macro view (big picture) of an instructional sequence. The micro view of stimulus-response-feedback (SRF) applies within each stage of the model. Here's how. Anything important that we show or tell the learner (stimulus, or S) should be checked out by getting a response, or R, from the learners to see that they understood and can apply the new information. We then owe them feedback, or F, on the appropriateness of their response. Now let's apply this rather brief lesson in educational psychology to the five items that relate to this competency.

In item 3, answers A and D are the best ways of measuring the course's effectiveness, since they test the learner's ability to apply what was taught. Answers B and C measure one's knowledge and verbal skills more than one's ability to close a sale.

In item 9, answers B and C are preferred, since they are the only two that follow the ADA model: lecture, examples to be critiqued, writing of letters.

Item 15 is concerned with breaking up a lecture, which is heavy on stimulus, by eliciting relevant responses from time to time. Answers A and D are good ways of doing this. In answer B the responses come too late to be useful, and in answer C, most learners will not respond.

In item 21, answers B and D are good. They elicit very relevant responses, require thought, and create a desire to learn by pinpointing needs. Answers A and C contain biased wording that can embarrass or annoy participants.

Evaluating Your Instructional Competencies

Item 27 is like item 9 in that it applies the three-stage learning model in answer A, which is correct. It also applies the SRF concept in answer C, which is correct. Answers B and D are not sufficient reasons for using films in a training program.

Instructing in both the inductive and deductive modes. Most of the instruction we have received—in school, at work, in scouts or clubs—made use of the inductive method of instruction. That is, the teacher told us new things and then tested our understanding by asking questions. In contrast, the deductive method makes use of questions and situations to lead the learners to discover, or deduce, the principles and concepts that are being taught. The inductive method is appropriate when students bring little or no prior knowledge or experience to the learning situation, such as in the teaching of a foreign language. But in the teaching of adults, their collective repertoire of experience is often rich and lends itself to the deductive method (also known as the Socratic or discovery method).

An effective instructor is skilled in the use of both methods and knows when to use each. The selection of each method depends not only on the learner's entering behavior, as just noted, but also on the course objectives, or terminal behaviors. For example, if we wish to teach students how to think for themselves in areas where there are no clear-cut, text-book solutions, then the deductive method is better for shaping this behavior. It's also better in developing attitudes. However, in teaching skills or procedures that are black-and-white and must be followed to the letter, the inductive method is better.

Item 4 is concerned with attitude change. The deductive method of answers B and C is better in getting the class to look at both sides of the new policy. They are thus more likely to accept it than if they feel it is being forced on them (induced), as in answers A and D.

In item 10, your responsibility is to the 16 employees who are inexperienced. If you play to the four who are more experienced and will answer more often (answers B and D), you will alienate and fail to meet the needs of the 16. Thus, answers A and C are preferred.

In item 16, the entering behavior of the group is high. Also, the course deals with how to supervise, which is situational in nature (relatively few black-and-white rules, and a high need for supervisors to weigh each situation and deduce the best way of handling it). These are reasons for teaching deductively—answers C and D.

Item 22 addresses the fact that when you teach deductively, students won't always give you what you're looking for, and it is your responsibility to rephrase questions and help students think through the consequences of their inappropriate responses. Thus, answers A and D are correct. Deductive instruction requires patience and flexibility, which are lacking in answers B and C.

In item 28, answers B and C are correct. The problem with A and D is the danger of having the blind lead the blind. If George is not as well versed as he'd like to be, he will have much better control of the group with answers B and C.

Maintaining adult (not parent-to-child) relationships in class. Most of the instruction we have experienced came from 12 years of public

213

school education in which we filled the dependent child role, and the teacher filled the parent role—at times judgmental and at times nurturing. Trainers who instruct employees must break with the parent-to-child model and teach on an adult-to-adult basis. Participants are not dependent on the trainer for grades, for knowing what they need to know, for sanctions and approval. Training will be far more effective and enjoyable when it is conducted on an adult-to-adult basis and not allowed to lapse into parent-to-child relationships. The five items that deal with this competency are concerned with problem participants and how the instructor should deal with them.

In item 5, answers B and D are correct, since they are adult ways of dealing with the situation. The problem with answers A and C is that they are likely to embarrass the participants—to scold them or put them down, which is typical parent-to-child behavior. Two results are likely: The participants will either withdraw and become inactive, or they will look for ways to strike back and even the score.

Item 11 tells you that a participant has tuned out. You should regard this as a symptom of a potential problem (topic is not relevant, too much talk and not enough participation). Thus, your appropriate responses are answers A and D. The risk associated with B and C is that they (a) assume Joe is the problem, and (b) he should be punished.

In item 17, the issue is one of how to deal with a disruptive participant. Answers C and D are adult-to-adult ways of handling it. In answers A and B, the instructor is filling the judgmental parent role.

In item 23, you want to do two things: get a reading on Nancy (which answer B does) and encourage her to contribute (which answer D does). You do not want to embarrass her or put her down, which could easily happen with answers A and C.

In item 29, answers A and D are the adult-to-adult way of getting people to sit with new neighbors, while B and C are parent-to-child.

The diagram below shows the "OK corral," in which we see the four states of "okays": Parent, Adult, Child, and Sick. When you teach in the parent state, your students are likely to respond from their child state. But when you teach in the adult state, your participants are much more likely to respond as adults. The comparison of parent and adult instructors is illustrated in the chart on the next page.

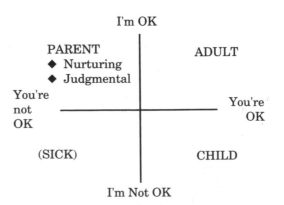

WHICH KIND OF INSTRUCTOR ARE YOU?

	PARENT-TO-CHILD RELATIONSHIPS	ADULT-TO-ADULT RELATIONSHIPS
Instructor's view of the mission	Learning is difficult and unpleasant for many. We must serve as a policeman or nurse to get learners through the lessons.	Learning can be satisfying and challenging—a major opportunity to test one's talents and develop them more fully.
Instructor's view of learners	Learners are dependent on the instructor to help them and to do most of the work.	Learners want to learn. They are capable of making decisions, solving problems, and setting goals for themselves if we let them.
Instructor's view of self	I'm OK, you're not OK. Trainees are too dependent on me. I end up having to do their thinking for them, and bailing them out.	I'm OK, you're OK. Once they've been trained, my role is that of a coach. I must step back and let them play the game.
Motivation used by instructor	Carrot and stick: set up system of rewards and punishments to entice and coerce learners.	The learning itself is inherently appealing; use it to give challenge, sense of achievement, recognition, responsibility, and growth.
Expectations: the Pygmalion effect	This instructor expects less of people than they are capable of—and gets it! "Expect the worst and you won't be surprised."	This instructor expects more of people than they knew they were capable of—and gets it! "Expect the best (not perfection) and people will give their best effort."
The working relationship	"Trainees are making my job (of teaching) easier or harder."	"I am making my trainee's job (of learning) easier or harder."
Motivation of trainees	They spend most of their energy keeping the instructor happy, harvesting the carrots, and avoiding the stick.	They invest their time meeting goals and standards that they and the instructor have agreed to jointly.

Staying learner centered, not information centered. This competency is concerned with your perception of the primary role of an instructor: whether it is to improve performance or to impart information. The former type of instructor is learner centered and sees the imparting of information as a means to this end. In contrast, the information-centered instructor sees the mission primarily as one of covering a lot of information within the time allotted for class. Some instructors are hired primarily to impart information and to function as an expert, like the typical college professor. But in the field of training, instructors are primarily responsible for improving the performance of their trainees. A learner-centered orientation is much more effective in accomplishing this than is the information-centered outlook. Let's apply this to the five applicable items in the assessment.

In item 6, answers A and C are learner centered and preferred. Answers B and D are more concerned with the instructor's needs than with the learner's.

In item 12, answers A and D are correct. They start class by assessing the needs of the learners in nonthreatening ways. In contrast, answer B is threatening, and C is information centered and premature until we find out more about their needs.

In item 18, the preferred answers are A and D because they focus on the learner and the receiving end of instruction. Answers B and C focus on the instructor and the sending end of the instructional process.

Item 24 presents the dilemma of how to deal with a wide range of abilities and work rates. Answers B and D are desirable ways of dealing with the problem. Answer A assumes that more information will cure the problem, though we have no evidence to suggest that comprehension is the problem. And answer C tries to get everyone to end up at the same time, which is not what the problem is.

In item 30 you need to find out if the student's need is one that other participants are having trouble with. You also need to diagnose where the student got lost in your earlier treatment of the topic. Answers A and D are good in accomplishing this. Answers B and C are information centered and guilty of assuming that more information will cure the problem.